ASHMOLEAN H

WATCHES

IN THE ASHMOLEAN MUSEUM

DAVID THOMPSON

ASHMOLEAN MUSEUM

2007

First published in the United Kingdom in 2007 by the Ashmolean
Museum, Publications Department, Beaumont Street,
Oxford OX1 2PH

ISBN 10: 1 85444 218 X (paperback) ISBN 13: 9 781854 442185
ISBN 10: 1 85444 219 8 (hardback) ISBN 13: 9 781854 442192

Titles in this series include:
Ruskin's drawings
Worcester porcelain
Maiolica
Drawings by Michelangelo and Raphael
Oxford and the Pre-Raphaelites
Islamic ceramics
English embroideries
Indian paintings from Oxford collections
Camille Pissarro and his family
Eighteenth-century French porcelain
Miniatures
Samuel Palmer
Twentieth-century paintings
Ancient Greek pottery
English Delftware
J. M. W. Turner
Glass of four millennia
Finger rings
Frames and framing
French drawings and watercolours
Scythian and Thracian antiquities
Japanese decorative arts of the Meiji period

David Thompson has asserted his moral right to be identified as the
author of this work

British Library Cataloguing in Publication Data
A catalogue record for this book is available from the British Library

Designed and typeset in Goudy by Geoff Green
Printed and bound in Singapore by Craft Print International Ltd

Contents

for Pam

With many thanks to Sir Harry & Lady Carol Djanogly

Acknowledgements

While this book comes from my reassessment of the Ashmolean Museum watch collections, it nevertheless owes a great debt to Gerald Taylor, former Senior Assistant Keeper in the Department of Western Art, whose earlier hand-list provided much valuable information relating especially to the decorative aspects of the watches and clocks. My special thanks go to my friend and colleague Timothy Wilson, Keeper of the Department of Western Art, for all his support and encouragement in the project. I am also grateful to all the staff of Western Art who, over the years, have welcomed me, made me coffee and generally looked after me on my visits to Oxford, especially Julie Arnott, Wendy Heppell, Bridget Allen, Sabrina Shim, and particularly Catherine Casley whose help in more recent years has been invaluable. My thanks also go to the staff in the Print Room for putting up with the strange man in the corner peering at watches through an eyeglass and muttering to himself.

No book of this sort is worth its salt with words alone. Without the illustrations it would not exist and my thanks and admiration go to David Gowers who has taken the photographs to bring the watches to life. Photographing shiny round objects with glass in them is never an easy task, but David has done these beautiful objects proud.

In the final process of producing this book thanks are also due to Emily Jolliffe for keeping the text under control and to Geoff Green for the overall design and layout. A special thanks must also go to my friend Andrew James for painstakingly reading the text and saving the author a number of red-face moments.

I am also grateful to my colleague Richard Edgcumbe

at the Victoria and Albert Museum, for his help and advice on 18th-century gold chasers and their work and to Philip Priestley for his time and information relating to the English watch case makers of the late 17th and early 18th centuries.

As she is in all my work, my wife Pam has been a tower of strength and a constant support in editing my words and making so many useful suggestions. I also express sincere thanks to my colleagues at the British Museum, Jeremy Evans, Paul Buck, and John Leopold for their support, advice, and suggestions. My final thanks go to Sir Harry Djanogly for his generous help towards the production of this book.

I hope that I have described the watches in such a way that they are accessible to those who have no horological knowledge, and that the book will be an encouragement to everyone to look at all the watches in the museum's wonderful collections and to see and enjoy them with a more informed eye.

Introduction

From the early years of the 16th century to the modern quartz precision era, watches have always been very personal and special to their owners, a fact borne out by their common use as Christmas, birthday, and anniversary gifts. However, it was not until the middle of the 19th century that old watches began to be seriously collected as part of a new fashion for antiquarians such as Debruge-Dumesnil, Ralph Bernal, and Octavius Morgan, who acquired them not simply as works of decorative art, but also as examples of technological advance. This passion for collecting watches has continued and developed and is still practised today.

The watches in the Ashmolean Museum collections are largely the result of three major bequests. Firstly that of Bentinck Hawkins, who left an important collection of portrait miniatures, objects of art, and watches to his brother Dr Bissett Hawkins with the intention that the collection would be presented to the University of Oxford when he died, and bequeathed in his late brother's name. The Bentinck Hawkins collection thus came to the museum in 1894 and it includes a group of fine large-sized coach watches and a small group of travelling clocks.

John Francis Mallett

John Francis Mallett (1875–1947) was born John Francis Snook but following his marriage he adopted his wife Margaret's surname. In 1909 he joined his father-in-law's business dealing in antiques and precious stones in Bath. The business expanded rapidly and in 1910 a London showroom was opened. The success of the London shop resulted in the Bath shop being closed in 1937 and everything moved to London, where the firm continues to this day. As well as running the family business, J. Francis Mallett built up his own private collections and when he died in 1947, 125 watches, along with medieval ivories, Limoges enamels, and fine porcelain, were bequeathed to the Ashmolean Museum. Now, the Mallett watches are considered to be one of the foremost collections of decorative material of the 17th century to be found in Britain.

Eric Bullivant had been a friend of Mallett's, and in 1974 his bequest of 120 watches came to the Ashmolean Museum. When these were added to Mallett's collection and those of Bentinck Hawkins, the Ashmolean Museum became home to one of the most important collections of watches to be found outside the national collections in London. Eric Bullivant's watches enhanced the Museum's collections by the addition of many fine 18th-century watches, complementing the strengths in earlier material in the Mallett bequest. Although the watches do not show the development of technical horology par-ticularly well, they display in considerable depth the his-tory and development of watch design and decoration, with examples of the art of the goldsmith, engraver, chaser, enameller, and lapidary from the mid-16th to the mid-19th century.

The Origins of the Watch

The watch has its origins at the beginning of the 16th century. By the end of the preceding century small portable clocks were becoming relatively common fol-lowing recent advances in the making of small coiled springs strong enough to drive the light movements. By simply miniaturizing the movement and lightening the case, as well as providing it with a cover to protect the dial and a pendant and ring so that it could be worn on the person, makers brought the watch into being. Although there is some evidence to suggest that there were watches in northern Italy at the end of the 15th century, there is no doubt that they were introduced in a serious way in South Germany at the beginning of the 16th century in centres such as Augsburg, Munich, and Nuremberg. At this time, watches were expensive luxury items usually worn suspended on a chain or ribbon around the neck and were commonly of drum or tambour shape but sometimes, more rarely, spherical. They probably served as much as demonstrations of wealth as they did as timekeepers.

Watches of spherical form dating from the middle of the 16th century are some of the earliest survivors and one of them, a small timepiece, is the first watch described in the book (no. 1). Even with its new dial, it is still a rare and important piece from the early history of the watch.

The small number of stackfreed watches in the museum's collections are all of German origin and are housed in the more common drum-shaped or tambour cases. These cases were made of gilded brass, cast, chased, and engraved with foliate designs, sometimes incorporating animals and hunting subjects, to enhance their opulence. In the early period, the movements were of steel, as brass at the time was relatively more expensive and unreliable as a structural metal when submitted to the stresses caused by the force of the mainspring. In order to combat the problem of rust, the steel was sometimes burnished. As machines for telling the time these watches were poor performers – indeed, a variation of as much as half an hour per day would have been considered good – but more importantly, they were erratic in their performance. However, the owners of these complicated machines were probably not, in the main, concerned with the time of day in hours, minutes, and seconds as we are today, and watches were probably not generally worn all day but were reserved by most for special occasions.

The main cause of inaccuracy was the variation in power output of the mainspring as it unwound to drive the watch. A coiled spring produces its greatest energy when fully wound and its energy output lessens progressively as the spring uncoils. Because the balance in early watches before the introduction of the balance spring had no natural period of swing, its rate of oscillation was determined by its mass, its radius, and the force exerted on it by the escapement. This meant that, without some means of evening out the changing force exerted by the mainspring, via the train of gears and the escapement, on the oscillating balance, the watch would gain drastically at the beginning of its run and lose significantly towards the end. To ensure reasonable accuracy, watchmakers in Germany introduced the stackfreed, a strong spring with a roller at its free end which acted on a snailed cam geared to the mainspring arbor, pushing against the mainspring to lessen its force at the beginning of the run and acting with the mainspring at the end of its run to augment its failing power.

One of the most spectacular of the stackfreed watches is the combined watch and astronomical compendium in the form of a book by Hans Koch of Munich, one of the most accomplished makers of his time (no. 4).

In the Germanic states, as the 16th century progressed, the shape of the watch changed from the drum-shape to a more rounded shape which lent itself more readily to the fashion of wearing the watch as a pendant. By the end of the 16th century smaller watches were much in vogue in oval and elongated octagonal shapes but the circular form continued to be popular, particularly in the mid-17th century. At this time watches were often made with an alarm, a type which continued until the end of the 17th century. In addition to watch cases made from gilded brass, cases made from rock crystal, with delicate frames to support them, became the height of fashion. Also, by the third quarter of the 16th century, steel became obsolete as a metal for movement plates and gear wheels, being universally replaced by brass.

no. 4

In the early years of the 17th century watch-making flourished in South Germany and many of the workshops were prolific in their output. The onset of the Thirty Years War in 1618, however, had a dramatic effect on the industry, as it not only severely hampered trade in central Europe but also eliminated members of the watch-buying aristocracy; those who survived were probably spending their money on weapons and war rather than on expensive luxuries. Watch-making in Germany nevertheless continued in the 17th century and into the next but it was never again to reach the status held by the celebrated makers of Augsburg, Nuremberg, and Munich during the 16th and early 17th centuries.

France and the Low Countries

By the middle of the 16th century, watch-making had spread northward and westward from the South German centres to France and the Low Countries. While some of the traditional skills were retained in these countries, they also added ideas of their own to the art, giving each country its particular characteristics. In place of the stackfreed, the favoured method of reducing the inconsistencies of the mainspring output was the fusee, a mechanism with obscure origins in 15th-century clocks. The mainspring was usually housed in a round drum or barrel and was provided with set-up and stop-work to enable the winding of the fusee to result in the winding of only the middle turns of the mainspring. Thus when the watch was fully wound the gut line, pulled by the force of the mainspring in its barrel, pulled on the smallest diameter of the fusee, and when the watch was almost run down, the gut line pulled on the largest diameter. During the run of the watch the gut line followed the curve of the fusee so that the changing force exerted by the mainspring on the gut line was matched with the relevant diameter of the fusee to equalize the torque exerted on the first wheel of the gear train, the wheel usually called the great wheel.

In the Low Countries, particularly Flanders, the watch-making tradition derived to some extent directly from the Germanic tradition. The popular form of watch was a large oval or round cased watch running for a whole day at one wind. These watches were generally enclosed in gilt metal cases engraved with foliate motifs, geometric designs, and pictorial scenes frequently taken from biblical sources or from mythology. By the early years of the 17th century watches in the Netherlands were more commonly in round, oval, or elongated octagonal cases, much smaller than their predecessors and having a running time of only sixteen hours. The 'furniture' on the back plates of the movements was usually finely pierced and engraved with foliate scrolls. A fine example of this genre can be seen in the form of a superbly made oval watch with calendar made in Haarlem in 1607 by Jan Janssen Bockelts (no. 6).

In France, the development of the watch is somewhat similar to that in the Low Countries. The early history of watch-making in France remains obscure, but by about 1560–70 they were being made in some numbers. In France, compared to their Flemish counterparts, watches were generally smaller and more delicate. Cases were enhanced with engraved floral decoration, often augmented with biblical or mythological subjects. Some of the finest watches were made in the great centres of Paris, Blois, Rouen, and Lyon. In the Ashmolean collections there are fine examples by French makers of the first half of the 17th century such as Pierre Combret of Lyon (no. 8) and Abraham Gribelin of Blois (no. 9), the latter's containing a small sundial in the case-back.

One major development in the appearance of the watch was that of pictorial painting in enamel. There had been watches decorated with simple designs in *en-basse-taille* enamel earlier in the century both in

no. 14

France and in Germany. However, it was Jean Toutin and his son Henri who developed the spectacular technique of painting in enamel in Châteaudun in France in the 1630s and later in Blois. By the middle of the 17th century the French workshops were producing a profusion of superb watch cases painted with subjects taken from mythological and, more commonly, biblical sources. Paris became a prolific centre for the making of these watch cases. A particularly fine example by Auguste Brettonneau shows the level of skill acquired by the French enamellers (no. 14). There are also a number of examples which show that trade in these luxurious cases was flourishing in England, using cases imported from France.

The Wars of Religion in France, beginning with the St Bartholomew's Day Massacre of 1572, and the subsequent persecution of Protestant Huguenots during the 17th century culminated in the exodus of Huguenots following the Revocation of the Edict of Nantes in 1685. This led to a decline in watch-making in France, and it is therefore not surprising to find that by the end of the century many Huguenot watchmakers and engravers had moved either to Geneva or London.

England

There is no evidence of the existence of any watchmakers in England before about 1560, and at that time those who were practising the craft were largely immigrants from the Low Countries and from Huguenot centres in France. Surviving examples of watches from this period show their close relationship with watch-making in the Flemish tradition. A maker such as Francis Nawe from Brabant had learned his craft before coming to London and continued to make watches in the way in which he had been accustomed. The native Englishmen who took up the craft were largely influenced by this tradition and their work shows many similar characteristics. By the early years of the 17th century, however, an English style had begun to develop. The large, whole-day-duration watches became obsolete and smaller watches grew in popularity, either in oval, elongated octagonal, or round cases, the last of these invariably used for alarm- and clock-watches, and their cases were often engraved with biblical or mythological subjects. By about 1620 the Flemish tradition was largely obscured by a powerful French influence following the establishment of a large group of Huguenot watchmakers in the environs of London, who brought with them highly developed skills in engraving and metal decorating techniques. Perhaps a measure of the popularity of all things French in the English court of James I was the invitation to David Ramsay, a Scot by birth, to return from France to become Royal Clockmaker in 1613. One example of a Ramsay watch in this book has a case which was either made in England in the French taste or, perhaps more likely, imported from France, given Ramsay's connections there (no. 7).

no. 7

In the 1630s the so-called 'form watch' became a fashionable type. Instead of the usual round, oval, or elongated octagonal shape for the case, watches were housed in a wide variety of fancifully shaped cases, based on the form of other objects. Cases in the form of a crucifix were common, and there are seven examples in the Ashmolean Museum. Sea shells and sea urchins abounded, as did floral shapes such as the tulip and the fritillary. Another common form was the human skull as a *memento mori*.

Such frivolous and obvious manifestations of wealth and status could do nothing but offend the principles of the Puritans living in mid-17th-century England. In order to satisfy the Puritan ethic, plain and simple designs were introduced, today termed 'Puritan', in which the silver or gilt-brass watch, round or more

commonly oval, would bear no exterior decoration and have only a simple chapter ring engraved on the dial. A watch by Edward East is typical except for the fact that the case is of gold, a metal rarely used for watch cases until the third quarter of the 17th century (no. 12).

In the period following the Great Plague and Great Fire of London in 1665 and 1666, the watch began to take on a more modern and more modest form. The introduction of the pocket in clothing, and the influence of the Puritan style led to the watch generally being a more modestly decorated item intended to tell the time rather than to be worn as an outward sign of wealth. There were, of course, still those who wished to demonstrate their riches but in the main watches took on a new character, which was enhanced by the introduction of the balance spring in 1675–6.

Switzerland

By the mid-16th century there is ample documentary evidence for the existence of watchmakers in Geneva. The art of the goldsmith and silversmith was highly developed there, and it should come as no surprise to find that some of the craftsmen turned their skills towards watch-making. A generation later the craft in Switzerland also benefited from the Huguenot refugees who settled in Geneva having fled persecution in France. The Swiss makers favoured styles more closely allied in character to the French tradition than to the Germanic style, although in some areas, such as Zug, Zurich, and Schaffhausen in the north, their watches were much more closely related to those of their near neighbours in Germany.

With a long tradition of gold and lapidary work in Geneva, it is not surprising that watches from Switzerland in the 17th century are frequently found in finely made rock crystal and other hard-stone cases as well as in enamel cases of fine quality. In the second half of the century the art of pictorial painting in enamel was taken to a new level of excellence in the work of the Huaud family. Pierre Huaud, the father, went to Geneva from Châtellerault in France and founded a dynasty of enamellers famed for their painted enamel watch cases. Following the establishment of the art by Jean Petitot in Geneva, the most celebrated and prolific of the later enamellers were Pierre Huaud the younger and his two brothers Jean Pierre and Amy Huaud whose cases can be found on the watches of various makers including a number in the Netherlands.

The invention of the balance spring in London led to a fundamental change in the use of watches. Although to some extent the Puritan style had produced watches which were generally objects for time measurement rather than simply status symbols or items of jewellery, it was the introduction of the balance spring which transformed the watch into a machine in which timekeeping was of prime importance. Indeed, the accuracy of the watch was greatly improved by the new invention. Watches before this momentous step forward in technology might keep time to within one half-hour per day, but a watch with a balance spring would be expected to measure time to within a minute per day or perhaps even less.

The change which the balance spring brought about was a huge step towards accurate timekeeping in the portable timekeeper. While the un-sprung balance had no natural period of oscillation and varied in its frequency depending on the amount of impulse it received from the escapement, the application of the balance spring to the balance meant that, within certain limits, the balance would take no longer to swing through long arcs than it would short arcs. The restoring force of the balance spring accelerates the balance back to the zero position faster when the balance rotates through the greater arc resulting from a bigger impulse from the escapement and consequently takes the same time.

By the time of the introduction of the balance spring the fusee reigned supreme as the device for evening out the variations in torque produced by the mainspring. One essential change had, nonetheless, taken place. Instead of a gut line to connect the mainspring barrel to the fusee, a small chain, rather like a bicycle chain in miniature, became the norm. The increased strength of these chains over the weaker gut lines allowed watch-makers to use a longer gear train of four wheels and make watches which would go for a whole day on a single wind. This was in stark contrast to the earlier watches with a gut line and a three wheel train which would normally go for about 15 or 16 hours on one wind.

The London Watchmakers

If watch-making expertise in the pre-balance spring era can be said to have been dominated by the makers of Germany, France, Flanders, and the Netherlands, the rise to domination of the London watchmakers can be traced through the 17th century. By the time the pendulum was introduced as an isochronous controller in clocks in 1657, English makers had already begun to develop an identifiable style. This is equally true of watches in the second half of the 17th century and particularly so in the period following the introduction of the balance spring in 1675. At this time relative affluence in England and well-established skills in watch and clock making led to London becoming the foremost centre of the art in Europe. Towards the end of the century, the expulsion of large numbers of Huguenot watchmakers from France undoubtedly had a beneficial influence on watch-making in London, particularly in the field of case making and decoration. The end of the 17th century and the beginning of the 18th century saw the growth of London as the capital of the watch-making world where many of the most accomplished craftsmen lived and worked. The Ashmolean collections are rich in examples of the fine work associated with that period of watch-making. The watch by the Huguenot watchmaker, Daniel Le Count (no. 18), is typical of the time.

The most celebrated of English clock and watchmakers is Thomas Tompion, whose watches were purchased and worn by many members of the aristocratic and noble families of Europe. Such was Tompion's fame during his lifetime that even then less honest makers were forging his work and name. In contrast to these dubious fakes, the Tompion watch included in this book is a fine example with a superb case signed and dated Abraham Martin 1683 (no. 19).

Of particular note is perhaps the earliest example of a watch with quarter repeat made by Daniel Quare of London (no. 21). It is very likely that this is the watch which Quare submitted to King James II in 1687 in competition with Thomas Tompion for a patent for his newly invented repeating mechanism. This new invention allowed the owner, by depressing a pendant in the case, to hear the watch strike the last hour and quarter on a bell.

This same period saw the introduction of a multitude of different forms of dial indication and the use of the 'mock-pendulum' balance which were eye-catching ways for the watchmakers of the time to attract customers in an environment of growing competition between the established London makers and the newly arrived Huguenots from France. A typical example is the watch with sun-and-moon dial by Richard Colston, made in about 1685 (no. 20).

The 18th century saw the introduction and rise in popularity of the *repoussé* pair-case. The Ashmolean collections have fine examples by the leading artists of the time. A finely chased case decorated by George

no. 18

no. 19

no. 20

no. 22

no. 28

no. 30

Michael Moser can be seen on a quarter repeating watch by George Graham of London (no. 25). Another example, a watch by Ellicott of Royal Exchange, London, has a case with an *en-suite* chatelaine; the case back follows a design by Augustin Heckel (no. 22).

In the 18th century, there were also developments in the export of watches to the Ottoman Empire, and in the third quarter of the century, the export of watches to China, a trade which continued well into the 19th century. The gold and enamel cased duplex watch made in Fleurier, Switzerland, for William Ilbery of London in about 1810 and intended for the Chinese market shows the style at its best (no. 28). In a quite different style is the gold and enamel triple cased watch made in about 1820 by Edward Prior for export to the Ottoman Empire (no. 30). Today, clocks and watches made for this market are commonly referred to as 'Turkish market', largely because the trading centre was Istanbul, although they were destined for a much wider area covering the whole of North Africa and through the Middle East.

The influence of the Huguenots was still apparent in the business of case making. Such was the change in fortune of the second- and third-generation Huguenots in London that, unlike their forebears in the early part of the 17th century who were not readily accepted by the establishment, in the 1680s the newly-arrived makers were accepted into the Clockmakers' Company as Free Brothers. Because they had already learnt their craft elsewhere, they were not permitted to take apprentices but many of them flourished and established successful workshops and more than one of them served as Master of the Clockmakers' Company. Others made their homes in Covent Garden and in Soho where they did not need to belong to a livery company in order to trade. A magnificent example of later 18th-century work can be seen in the watch by Thomas Mudge & William Dutton (no. 27), made in the 1770s and housed in a gold and enamel case by the Huguenot, Peter Mounier.

France in the 18th Century

The history and development of watch-making in areas except London in the 18th and 19th centuries is not well reflected in the collection, but worthy of note are a typical French *oignon* style verge watch made in about 1690 by François Rabby of Paris (no. 17) and a gold and enamel cased watch by Ferdinand Berthoud, also of Paris, made in 1769 (no. 26). One of the most celebrated of all watchmakers was Abraham Louis Breguet who founded a watch-making firm which continues to this day. The Ashmolean collections contain five watches from the Breguet workshops. The one chosen for this book is a typical Breguet *montre à tact* (no. 29) made in about 1820, in which the time can be ascertained by feeling the position of the hand in relation to raised studs at the hours around the outside of the case.

no. 27

no. 17

The Coach Watch

Finally, mention should also be made of the fine collection of large-size coach watches made for use by travellers during the 17th and 18th centuries. One place particularly famed for the manufacture of these watches was Friedberg, a small town near Augsburg in Bavaria, where in many instances the makers added the word 'London' to their signatures on the movements to enhance the status of their work. Typical of the Friedberg and Augsburg workshops is the watch by Andreas Grundler (no. 23).

no. 23

WATCHES

1. Anonymous

Spherical cased verge clock-watch with stackfreed
German, *c.*1540

Case: diameter 45.5 mm, height
50.5 mm
Movement: diameter 40.5 mm,
pillar height 6.4 mm

Provenance:
Formerly in the Albert Schloss
Collection, sold Christie's, London,
16 April 1920, lot 111.
J. Francis Mallett Bequest, 1947
(WA1947.191.1)

Literature:
Baillie, 1929, pl.VI, no.1, pp.55, 93.

Although the identification of the earliest watches
remains a difficult task, it is now generally agreed that
the small group of examples which are housed in spherical cases may well be some of the earliest survivors. It is
very likely that these spherical watches relate closely to
the perfume pomanders which were popular in the first
half of the 16th century. A particularly interesting reference exists from 1524 in which Peter Henlein of
Nuremberg was paid 15 florins for a gilded musk apple
the whole thing with a watch.

This example, although unsigned, was undoubtedly
made in Germany in the early to mid-16th century. The
gilt-brass spherical case, chased with strap-work and
arabesques, has the dial at the bottom. Unfortunately,
this dial is not original. Although it has a chapter ring
with hours I–XII and floral half-hour marks surrounding
the characteristically Germanic Arabic hours 13–24, the
circle around the middle divided into five-minute inter-
vals shows it to be a modern replacement. A single-
handed watch from this period would have had a dial
only divided into quarter hours.

The movement is constructed from iron in two stages,
with three plates and chamfered pillars to support the
wheels and pinions of the gear trains. The going train is
mounted above the striking train and, in typical
Germanic style for the period, a stackfreed mechanism is
used to equalize the decreasing power produced by the
mainspring as it unwinds. The striking train is controlled
by a count-wheel with a so-called 'nag's head' release
operated by twelve-point star-wheel mounted on the dial
wheel under the dial. The bell is mounted inside the top
half of the case. The lack of screws in the movement and

the fact that the mainsprings are not housed in barrels, as they are in later watches, confirm an early date of pre-1550 for the watch.

At some time in the past, this watch was subjected to some extreme conditions and in consequence the movement is now somewhat distressed. Another example of similar type, now in the Walters Art Museum, Baltimore, is the earliest dated watch known to survive. It was made in 1530 for the Protestant reformer, Philipp Melanchthon (1497–1560).

2. Anonymous

Tambour cased stackfreed watch (case and dial)
South Germany, c.1560–80

By the middle of the 16th century watches were becoming popular in South Germany, with watchmakers producing them in considerable numbers. Today these watches are relatively rare, and this example unfortunately survives only as a case and dial.

The cast gilt-brass case has a hinged lid to cover the dial and the integral back of the case is decorated with foliage and female figures. Around the middle, the case band has upper and lower mouldings enclosing a pierced frieze of foliate scrolls and animals. The lid is pierced out between a circle of caryatid figures to reveal the hour numerals on the dial beneath.

The chapter-ring is typically Germanic in style with the hours marked I–XII and 13–24 and with T-shaped half-hour marks surrounding a quarter-hour circle of alternate hatched and plain rectangles. In the centre is an engraved arabesque design. A hole at XI–XII is there to allow a peg to be inserted to release the striking to

Case: diameter 60.0 mm, thickness 24.0 mm.

Provenance:
Formerly in the Alain Collection (Paris).
J. Francis Mallett Bequest, 1947 (WA1947.191.3)

Literature:
Baillie, 1929, pl.VII, pp.55, 57, 94.

synchronize it with the time shown on the dial, a necessary task if the striking train ran out of power before the going.

The movement of this watch would have been made from iron and would have been furnished with a stack-freed to equalize the power of the mainspring. The fact that the case is pierced around the band shows it to have been a clock-watch striking the hours.

3. Anonymous

Gilt-brass cased verge clock-watch with alarm
South Germany, *c.*1580.

Case: diameter 61.6 mm, thickness
30.6 mm
Movement: diameter 46.6 mm,
pillar height 10.6 mm.

Provenance:
Formerly in the Percy Webster
Collection.
J. Francis Mallett Bequest, 1947
(WA1947.191.8)

Literature:
Baillie, 1929, pl.IX, pp.57, 61, 94.

As the 16th century progressed, watches became more
common in South Germany and by the third quarter
their shape had changed from the tambour to a more
rounded form. It was also in this era, from about 1580
onwards, that movement plates began to be made from
brass rather than iron. This watch has a cast, gilt-brass
case, chased on the back with a vase and floral scrolls.
The case band is pierced with foliate scrolls and the
cover is pierced in a geometric pattern with two circles
of twelve apertures to reveal the hour numerals beneath.
There is a small gilt-brass pendant with a loose ring for
attaching the watch to a ribbon or chain to allow it to be
worn around the neck.

The silver dial has hours numbered I–XII and 13–24 in
dark blue enamel, with a circle of alternate hatched and
plain rectangles for the quarters and the '2' numerals in
the typical German angular form. Around the outside, a
circle of touch-pins at the hours allows the watch to be
used in the dark, the pin at XII being higher and more
pointed. At VII o'clock there is a hole which facilitates the
release of the striking train to synchronize it with the time

shown by the hand. There is a gilt-brass alarm-setting disc numbered 1–12 in the middle of the dial. The blued-steel hand is a later replacement.

The movement strikes the hours and has an alarm. The gilt-brass stackfreed cam, with its engraved decoration on the top, is retained by a large quatrefoil washer. There is a key-operated hog's bristle regulator with a gilt-brass disc numbered 1–8 to enable fine adjustment to the timing of the watch. The striking train is controlled by a count wheel, and the alarm mechanism operates an oscillating hammer with a sliding block stop-mechanism to silence the alarm when necessary.

4. Hans Koch

Gilt-brass cased clock-watch with alarm, sundials and lunar volvelle in the form of a book
Munich, *c.*1580
Signed: HK with a monk's head

Case: length 100.6 mm (inc. pendant loop), width 68.2 mm, thickness 27.4 mm.
Movement: length 83.5 mm, width 52.4 mm, pillar height 8.4 mm.

Provenance:
J. Francis Mallett Bequest 1947
(WA1947.191.7)

Literature:
Baillie, 1929, pls. XXVIII and XXIX, p.124.
David Thompson, 'Watches in the Ashmolean Museum' *Antiquarian Horology*, 25 (Sept 2000), p.505.

In the 16th and 17th centuries, there was a fashion for the ownership of scientific instruments. The astronomical compendium, a number of different instruments combined in one case and small enough to be portable, became a highly desirable object; the more sophisticated it was, the more status it carried. This rare combination of a calendrical compendium and an hour-striking clock-watch with alarm was made by Hans Koch, one of the leading makers in South Germany at the time. His mark 'HK' conjoined within a shield, and a separate right-facing monk's head, the town mark of Munich, are punched on the back of the movement.

Two sundials and a lunar volvelle make up the compendium. The cast gilt-brass case in the form of a book has two closing latches on the open edge and a spine partially pierced and decorated with scrolling foliage and flowers. On the outside of the lid is a large manual

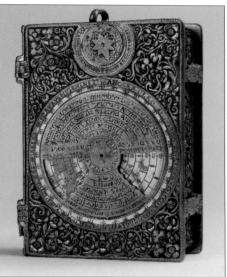

volvelle within a fixed circle engraved with degrees and signs of the zodiac. Around the volvelle are several place names in separate circles appropriate for their latitudes, numbered 42, 44, 46, 48, 50, and 52 and inscribed: GRAD:ELEVATIO:POLI (degree of polar elevation [latitude]). Around the centre is the inscription: QVANT: DIEI*QVANT:NOCT* (amount of day – amount of night). Two large apertures in the volvelle reveal concentric circles engraved with the number of hours of daylight and darkness. On the solid area between the apertures three points enclose the inscription: MOVEATVR INDEX.AD GRADVM SOLIS (the index may be moved for for the degree of the sun). In use, the volvelle is rotated until the index points to the appropriate date expressed in terms of degrees of a zodiac sign. The hours of daylight and darkness for that day can then be read next to the circle in which the required location is listed. At the top, a smaller roundel is inscribed: GRADVS. DECLINATIO.MAGNETIS (degree of magnetic declination) and calibrated with a scale. The central area of the roundel is formed by the

base of a compass box which is rotated to comply with the
required magnetic declination.

The inside of the lid has an adjustable horizontal sundial for use between latitudes 45° north and 52° north.
and below is a lunar volvelle with an aspectarium
engraved in the middle of a manually adjusted central
disc inscribed INDEX DIERVM AETATIS LVNAE (daily
index of the age of the moon). The scale beneath the disc
is divided 1–29½ for the age of the moon. A fixed scale
around the outside is divided I–XII twice and the scale
around the edge of the disc is calibrated in hours from 3
through 12 to 9, which more than covers all the times at
which the moon might cast a shadow in the latitudes for
which the compendium was designed to work. A circular
aperture in the disc shows the phase of the moon.

The main dial has a pin-gnomon sundial in the upper
part, with signs of the zodiac to the left and right showing unequal hours, with lines for the two tropics and the
equator, each named, and a dial inscribed DIEI HORAE
PLANET (planetary hours of the day). In the lower part,
the clock dial has a chapter ring with hours I–XII twice,

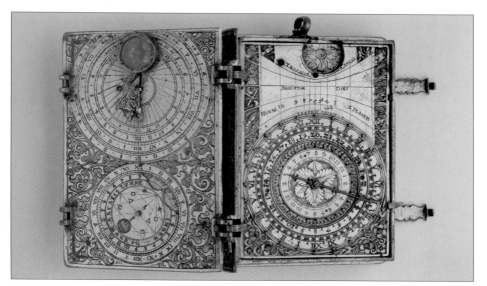

T-shaped half-hour marks, and alternate hatched and plain rectangles for the quarters. There are also touch pins at the hours. Within the fixed chapter ring is a manually adjusted ring numbered 1–24 to show hours such as Bohemian or Nuremberg, where the day begins at sunset or sunrise. In the centre, a disc numbered 1–12 twice allows for setting the alarm. The blued-steel hand is not original.

The watch movement has two quite separate mechanisms. The first is circular with gilt-brass plates and shaped pillars. The going train is powered by a fixed barrel with stackfreed. The four wheel going train of steel wheels drives a verge escapement with a steel dumb-bell balance. The rate of the balance is regulated by a hog's bristle regulator. The bristles are mounted on a long gilt-brass angled arm moved by turning the blued-steel hand on the gilt brass drum on the back plate, calibrated 1–9 for regulation. Also contained in this movement is the simple alarm mechanism. In a separate shaped movement at the top is the hour striking mechanism controlled by a gilt-brass count-wheel numbered 1–12.

5. Francis Nawe

Oval gilt-brass verge watch

London, *c.*1580

Signed: FRANCOIS * NAWE * AT * LONDEN

Case: length 86.9 mm, width
54.2 mm, thickness 30.5 mm.
Movement: length 61.4 mm, width
47.9 mm, pillar height 13.25 mm.

Provenance:
Formerly in the Levy Collection and
Percy Webster Collection, sold
Sotheby's, London, 27 May 1954,
lot 9 to T. P. Camerer Cuss.
Eric Bullivant Bequest, 1974
(WA1974.154)

Literature:
David Thompson, 'Watches in the
Ashmolean Museum', *Antiquarian
Horology*, 25 (Sept 2000),
pp.509–10.

By the end of the 16th century the art of watch-making had spread far and wide from South Germany, particularly into France and the Low Countries. In England, watch-making was still in its infancy, and to a large extent it was in the hands of Protestants from Flanders and the Netherlands who brought their skills across the English Channel in the 1570s. London was an affluent destination for those who wished to practise a luxury trade, as well as a place where Protestants could freely follow their religion. However, being foreign, the immigrants were not readily accepted into the London Livery Companies and thus were unable to establish businesses within the city boundaries. Instead, many settled in the Austin Friars and Blackfriars areas just outside the city walls. Francis Nawe was a member of this community, coming from Brabant and settling in Austin Friars where he worshipped at the Dutch Church.

This is a typical oval verge watch of the period, both in size and design, and its Flemish origins are clearly apparent. The style of engraved floral border around the edge of the back plate is one associated with English watch-making in the late Elizabethan period, a custom also occasionally found in Flanders at the time. The case lid depicts a woman with two urns and intertwined foliage with a canopy above. The back is engraved with a central urn, strap-work, and foliage incorporating a canopy and there is a scallop-shell cover to the winding hole. These engravings are after designs by Etienne Delaune (1518–83) whose engravings were a popular source for decoration at the end of the 16th century.

6. Jan Janssen Bockelts

Oval gilt-brass cased verge watch with calendar
Haarlem, 1607
Signed: Jan Janss Bockelts

Case: length 69.5 mm, width
48.9 mm, thickness 28.0 mm.
Movement: length 54.5 mm, width
42.5 mm, pillar height 10.3 mm.

Provenance:
Albert Schloss Collection.
Maurice Sternberger Collection,
sold Christie's, London,
22 November 1937, lot 84.
J. Francis Mallett Bequest, 1947,
(WA1947.191.13).

Literature:
David Thompson, 'Watches in the
Ashmolean Museum', *Antiquarian
Horology*, 25 (Sept 2000),
pp.507–8.

One of the most accomplished Dutch watchmakers was
Jan Janssen Bockelts the elder, originally from Aachen,
but known to have been working in Haarlem by 1607.

Engraved on the back of the case is a grisly depiction
of *Judith with the Head of Holofernes*, here executed in a
quality of engraving rarely found on watches. The dial
has emblematic figures, birds, and scrolls around
subsidiary dials. The lower centre dial shows the days
and months of the year. The age and phase of the moon
with the letters E for *eerst*, V for *vol*, L for *laatst*, and N
for *nieuw*, indicating the first quarter, full, last quarter,
and new phases of the moon are around the outside to
the upper left. The date 1–30 is shown in the upper right
subsidiary. In the centre, the applied silver chapter ring
has hours I–XII, star-shaped half-hour marks and an inner
circle with alternate hatched and plain marks dividing
each hour into eight parts or half-quarters.

The movement shows characteristics from two tradi-
tions, as one might expect of a maker from Aachen on
the border between the Germanic states and the Low
Countries. It is a fusee watch but here Bockelts has
incorporated a hog's bristle regulator, a device largely
associated with the Germanic tradition of watch-making,
for finely adjusting the rate of the watch.

As a final addition to the documentary nature of this
watch is the inscription on the inside of the back,
'*Abraham Ampe anno 1607*'. Ampe, a merchant in
Haarlem, who was 21 in 1607 when this watch was
made, is known to have been a close friend of Jan
Janssen Bockelts and it is possible that this watch could
have been a 21st birthday present from Bockelts.

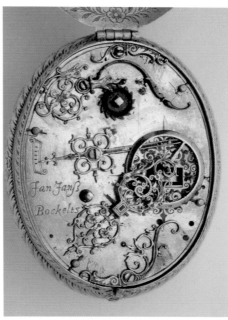

7. David Ramsay

Elongated octagonal gilt-brass and silver cased verge watch

London, *c.*1615

Signed: David Ramsay Scotus

Case: length 60.5 mm, width 34.5 mm, thickness 21.9 mm.
Movement: length 42.3 mm, width 30.85 mm, pillar height 8.9 mm.

Provenance:
Captain Plumtree Collection, stated to have been sold Sotheby's, London, 1930.
J. Francis Mallett Bequest, 1947, (WA1947.191.36)

This elongated octagonal watch has a gilt-brass case decorated with scenes from Ovid's *Metamorphoses* Book 3. A series of eight facets on the cover, engraved with foliate scrolls, surround a larger central panel depicting *Diana and Actaeon*. The back is decorated in a similar manner with a depiction of *Narcissus*. The applied silver band is engraved with foliate scrolls and rabbits; on the inside of the cover are the British royal arms with a three-barred label, the shield surmounted by a royal coronet and flanked by the letters 'P' and 'H'.

Foliate scrolls, birds, and squirrels decorate the dial with *Leda and the Swan* at the top and a female grotesque at the bottom. The gilt-brass chapter-ring is engraved with Roman hour numerals and star-shaped half-hour marks

surrounding a double inner circle with dots at the hours. The central area is engraved with a pastoral scene with a river and a town. The movement back-plate has an engraved border of foliate scrolls with rabbits around the edge but, apart from that, it has been extensively modernized at some time during the third quarter of the 18th century, the work executed in a very professional manner.

The Stuart arms and initials HP are those of Henry Prince of Wales, elder son of James I (d. 1612). The engraving of the letters HP is not, however, particularly elegant and the coronet is not that normally used by the heir apparent. It is possible that the shield of arms etc. have been added to enhance the importance of the watch. In the 19th century there were certainly some watch dealers who were less than scrupulous. As a result, a number of perfectly genuine watches from the Jacobean period gained shields of arms etc., to which they had no claim, and provenances which were unsubstantiated. There is no doubt, however, that some watches have a better claim to royal origins and it may be significant that there is a record that in 1612 Ramsay was paid £61 for three watches for the Prince of Wales.

8. Pierre Combret

Elongated octagonal gilt-brass and silver cased verge clock-watch

Lyon, *c.*1615–20

Signed: Pierre Combret

Case: length 68.3 mm, width 39.4 mm, thickness 28.0 mm.
Movement: oval, length 34.8 mm, width 28.4 mm, pillar height 9.39 mm.

Provenance:
Formerly in the Pilkington Collection (1851) 'Wonastin Heirlooms'.
Frank Partridge, 1944.
J. Francis Mallett Bequest, 1947 (WA1947.191.37)

In the first half of the 17th century, Lyon was one of the major centres of watch-making in France. One of the more accomplished makers working there was Pierre Combret the younger.

Made in about 1620, this example of his work has an elongated octagonal silver case in which the back consists of eight small panels, engraved with foliate scrolls, rabbits, and musicians surrounding a larger central panel decorated with a depiction of *Susanna and the Elders.* The silver front cover also has eight smaller panels engraved with foliate scrolls, fabulous animals, and nude figures around a larger central panel showing *Daniel Confounding the Elders.*

Reclining nude figures and foliate scrolls adorn the dial, on which is pinned a gilt-brass chapter-ring engraved with Roman hours and dot half-hour marks between two circles, with dots at the hours around the inner one. The area within the chapter-ring is engraved with a depiction of *The Stoning of St Stephen.* Such scenes taken from the Bible were popular as decoration on French watches of the first quarter of the 17th century .

The movement is also typical of the 1620s with a going period of about 16 hours from a single wind. This meant, of course, that in use the watch would have to be wound twice per day. As a clock-watch, in addition to indicating the time, the watch strikes the hours on an oval bell mounted in the back of the case.

9. Abraham Gribelin

Oval gilt-brass and silver cased verge clock-watch
with astronomical dial and sunrise–sunset table
Blois, *c.*1630
Signed: 'Gribelin Blois'

Of all of the accomplished watchmakers in Blois in the
first half of the 17th century it is probably Abraham
Gribelin who stands out as the maker of the most interesting and finely decorated watches. This wonderfully
ornate watch is housed in a case with cast and chased
silver panels of high quality, depicting *Orpheus Charming
the Animals* on the lid and *Minerva, Venus, and Juno* on
the back. The silver band around the case is also pierced
and engraved with foliate scrolls, grotesques, and

Case: length 83.1 mm, width 54.1
mm, thickness 31.9 mm.
Movement: oval, length 42.0 mm,
width 37.1 mm, pillar height 10.2
mm.

Provenance:
Formerly in the collection of
Captain G. H. Wilbraham, sold
Sotheby's, London, 9 March 1939,
lot 91
J. Francis Mallett Bequest, 1947
(WA1947.191.31)

Literature:
Gerhard König, *Die Uhr*, Berlin
1991, ill.57–60
David Thompson, 'Watches in the
Ashmolean Museum', *Antiquarian
Horology*, 25 (Sept 2000),
pp.512–14. figs. 24–29.

half-figures. Added to this impressive ensemble is a table of sunrise–sunset times for the year, appropriate for latitude 52–53° North. Blois is on a parallel slightly greater than 48° North, making it clear that the watch was made specifically for someone living in Northern Europe, perhaps Amsterdam.

The calendar dial shows the days of the week through an oval aperture at the bottom. A wide gilt-brass ring is engraved in concentric circles for the date, the months, and the degrees and signs of the zodiac. Within this ring is a silver chapter-ring with hours I–XII and arrow-head half-hour marks. The chamfered inside edge of the chapter-ring is calibrated 1–29½ for the age of the moon and a central gilt-brass disc is engraved with an aspectarium incorporating an aperture for the moon's phase. A steel pointer registers against the gilt-brass calendar ring and a central blued-steel hand shows the time.

The fine-quality movement is equal in quality to the case, with four baluster pillars separating the plates, a mainspring barrel with ratchet and click set-up on the back plate as well as a fusee and verge escapement. To add to the sophistication of this extremely fine watch, it strikes the hours.

10. Jean Baptiste Duboule

Silver cased verge watch in the form of a lion

Geneva, *c.*1635

Signed: Jean Baptiste Duboule

Case: length 47.65 mm, width 27.25 mm, height 38.35 mm.
Movement: shaped oval, length 33.35 mm, width 18.1 mm, pillar height 9.4 mm.

Provenance:
Formerly in the Dyson Perrins Collection.
J. Francis Mallett Bequest, 1947 (WA1947.191.54)

Literature:
F. J. Britten, *Old Clocks and Watches and their Makers*, 3rd edn. 1911, fig. 154, pp.146–8.

During the mid-17th century there was a fashion, particularly in Geneva, for watch cases in the form of animals, a small number of which survive. These include a watch signed Jean Baptiste Duboule in the form of a miniature silver dolphin with tiny ruby eyes. Another by Pierre Duhamel resembles a rabbit, a third by Jacques Jolly takes the form of a small dog, and yet one more by Henry Ester is a miniature swan.

This watch, by Jean Baptiste Duboule, has a case in the form of a cast lion with the movement and dial in the lion's belly. The movement front plate is engraved with foliate scrolls and flowers to surround an applied silver dial with hours I–XII, straight-line half-hour marks and dots at the hours, with an engraved landscape in the centre. Attached to the back of the dial is the small

watch movement with a fusee and verge escapement.

However beautiful this watch was and however desirable it would have been in Geneva, it was not to be worn there, as such ornaments were not allowed in the Calvinist city state in the 17th century. In the *Sumptuary Ordinances and Laws concerning Clothing, furnishings and other excesses of similar kinds*, reviewed by the Little Council and the Grand Council of the Republic of Geneva in February and June 1668, is the following: *Item: Women and girls are forbidden all gold needles and pins and all things made with precious stones on their dress and accoutrements…. all watchmakers' watches and mirrors at their girdles.* It is perhaps not surprising, therefore, to find that even earlier in the century makers like Duboule specialized in export material, with much of their work destined for Constantinople where, in the Ottoman Empire, watches like this would have been highly prized.

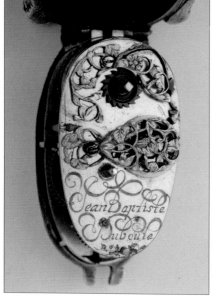

11. Zacherie Fonnereau

Silver cased verge watch

La Rochelle, *c.*1640

Signed: Fonnereau à La Rochelle

Case: diameter 36.75 mm, thickness 17.3 mm.
Movement: diameter 29.0 mm, pillar height 7.3 mm.
Overall length including chatelaine 172.2 mm.

Provenance:
Formerly in the Webster Collection.
J. Francis Mallett Bequest, 1947 (WA1947.191.62)

In France from the end of the 16th century the Wars of Religion split the country between the Catholic establishment and the Protestant Huguenots. Many of the Protestants had already migrated to cities such as Geneva and London to find religious freedom. Those Protestants who remained in France tended to congregate in communities, and La Rochelle was one of them. Zacharie Fonnereau ran a busy workshop there, judging from the fact that five watches survive bearing his name, and a further eight watches signed 'Fonnereau à La Rochelle' can be attributed to his workshop.

This silver watch has a round case engraved with eight radiating segments of natural flowers on the front and back. On the inside, the cover is engraved with the arms of the first owner, Wolmer of Kinton in Worcestershire, and the mottoes: *Gloria Nobilitati. non debita. sed. providentiae* (Glory is not due to nobility but to [divine] providence) and *amor mihi crescit in horas* (my love grows by the hour). With the watch is a three-strand silver chain with one decorated plate embossed with a crowned female bust.

The floral design of the case is continued in the form of an engraved border on the movement front plate, surrounding a silver dial with a chapter-ring with hours I–XII and arrow-head half-hours. The area within the chapter-ring is also engraved with realistic flowers. The central hand is not original. The movement of the watch is of standard design with a fusee with gut line connection to the mainspring barrel and a verge escapement with a balance oscillating beneath a finely pierced and engraved foliate balance cock.

12. Edward East

Oval gold cased verge watch

London, *c.*1645

Signed: Eduardus East Londini

Outer case: length 55.8 mm, width 49.9 mm, thickness 23.5 mm.
Inner case: length 57.4 mm, width 42.6 mm, thickness 23.2 mm.
Movement: length 41.4 mm, width 35.7 mm, pillar height 7.54 mm.

Provenance:
Formerly in the Harman Collection, 1933.
J. Francis Mallett Bequest, 1947 (WA1947.191.80)

In England and to some extent in the Netherlands in the mid-17th century a style of watch evolved which was expressly intended to appeal to members of the 'Puritan' movement. In contrast to the highly decorative watches in enamel cases and ornately engraved cases, these watches were completely devoid of any ornament. They were often housed in an outer container which when closed appeared from the outside as a plain metal box. Inside, the watches were also without decoration and had an aperture through which the time could be seen through a glass. Apart from watches housed in faceted rock-crystal, these were the first watches to have a glass in the front cover.

Typical of the 'Puritan' style, the plain gold case on this watch has an integral back and hinged glazed lid. On the back there is a rotating cover over the winding hole. The leather-covered brass case has gilt rims and gold piqué point decoration with a monogram on the back, probably the combination of the letters HARTVS with a letter S above and below, perhaps referring to the owner.

The dial is plain gold with an applied silver chapter-ring with Roman hours and arrow-head half-hours sur-rounding a quarter-hour circle. The time is shown by a single blued-steel hand with long tail.

The movement is without decoration apart from the pierced and engraved balance cock on the back plate and the name of the maker. To adjust the rate of the watch there is a key-operated tangent-screw mechanism which changes the 'set-up' of the mainspring and a silver index disc engraved 1–8, which acts as a reference.

13. Richard Crayle

Silver cased verge watch in the form of a tulip, London, *c.*1640

Signed: Richard Crayle Fecit

Case: length 39.4 mm, width 25.1 mm, thickness 26.1 mm. *Movement:* length 25.95 mm, width 21.4 mm, pillar height 6.4 mm.

Provenance:
Eric Bullivant Bequest, 1974 (WA1974.117)

In contrast to the 'Puritan' style of the preceding watch by Edward East, this watch has a silver case ornately cast in the form of a tulip bud. Watches of this type, now commonly referred to as 'form' watches, were made to resemble such forms as sea urchins, shells, rose buds, or even animals, as in the case of the watch by Jean Baptiste Duboule (no. 10).

In this instance, Richard Crayle has used a case with three hinged petals overlaid with symmetrical leaves to form the flower. Just who made these fine silver cases is not known. However, they certainly come from workshops which supplied a number of different watchmakers. Other similar, although not identical, examples are known which contain movements by Simon Hackett and Henry Grendon.

In a period when flowers were popularized by the new Dutch still-life paintings and Tulip Mania in the Netherlands had reached a peak in the 1630s, it is perhaps not surprising to find the tulip form used as a watch case.

The dial is also of silver, with a small blued-steel hand showing the time against an engraved chapter-ring with Roman hours, half-hour marks and a quarter-hour circle. Inside the chapter-ring is an engraved townscape, typical of English work of the mid-17th century.

The oval gilt-brass movement has four baluster pillars and tangent-screw set-up to adjust the rate of the small balance which oscillates beneath a pierced foliate balance cock pinned to the back plate.

14. Auguste Brettonneau

Gold and enamel cased verge watch, Paris, *c.* 1650
Signed: Auguste Brettonneau à Paris

Case: diameter 59.8 mm, thickness 18.8 mm.
Movement: diameter 50.7 mm, pillar height 6.8 mm

Provenance:
J. Francis Mallett Bequest, 1947 (WA1947.191.90)

Literature:
David Thompson, 'Watches in the Ashmolean Museum', *Antiquarian Horology*, 25 (Sept 2000), pp.515–16. figs.33–6.

Following the perfecting of the art of pictorial painting in enamel by Jean and Henri Toutin in the 1630s, the technique was quickly adopted by other artists, particularly in Blois and Paris. By the middle of the 17th century it had reached a prolific level of production and the enamellers were supplying large numbers of cases and dials to the watchmakers. The French case makers also found a ready market in London for these fabulous cases in which a movement could be installed for a rich customer of courtly rank.

This watch by Auguste Brettonneau of Paris, made in about 1650, is a particularly fine example of this wonderful form of decorative art. The enamel decoration on the inside of the case depicts *St Mary Magdalene* characterized by her ointment jar and her long flowing hair. The dial centre, within the chapter ring, is enamelled with a depiction of *St Catherine* with her attribute, the broken wheel. The religious theme is continued with *The Annunciation* inside the lid and *The Holy Family* on the outside of the back. Finally the outside of the cover is painted with a version of *The Visitation*. Here the movement is of a standard form of the period but now lacks the decorative ratchet click on the back plate.

The subjects for the decoration were usually taken from oil paintings or engravings by renowned artists of the time and perhaps the most popular of these was Simon Vouet (1590–1649). The results are quite astounding when it is realized that each colour requires a separate firing in the kiln. The unknown maker of this unsigned case had to be a goldsmith to make the box, an artist to realize the illustrations, a chemist to mix the enamels, and a master at controlling a kiln.

15. Leonhard Engelschalckh

Square cased verge watch

Friedberg, *c.*1660

Signed: Leonhard Engelschalckh

Case: 37.6 mm square, length
47.4 mm with pendant.thickness
14.3 mm.
Movement: 32.3 mm square, pillar
height 5.2 mm.

Provenance: Eric Bullivant
Bequest, 1974 (WA1974.207)

Literature:
Adelheid Riolini-Unger,
Friedberger Uhren, catalogue of an
exhibition of Friedberg clock- and
watch-making held at the Heimat
Museum, Friedberg, in 1993.

By the middle of the 17th century watch and clock making in the small town of Friedberg, near Augsburg in South Germany, had become very active. A number of families involved in the manufacture of clocks and watches were well established. The proximity to the city of Augsburg and its expertise in both clock making and fine metal working must have had an influence on the Friedberg industry.

This particular example is one of a small group of watches made with square cases in the mid-17th century. The fashion for these square-cased watches was perhaps at its most popular in St Germain, Paris, but there are also a small number of surviving watches made in South Germany, two by Johann Michael Keller of Friedberg and a third with a movement made by Siegmund Albrecht of Regensburg. The similarity between these watches suggests a case-maker or silversmith making cases of similar design for sale to watchmakers.

The square gilt-brass case has applied pierced silver foliate panels on all the faces, secured by screws at the corners. The insides of the case are also gilded. The front of the case forms the dial plate, which also has an applied silver pierced foliate panel *en-suite* with the case. Applied over the front plate is a gilt-brass chapter-ring with hours I–XII and with foliate half-hour marks between two engraved circles.

16. Estienne Ester

Serpentine, gold and enamel cased verge watch
Geneva, *c*.1670
Signed: Estienne Ester

Case: diameter 25.7 mm, thickness
15.5 mm.
Movement: diameter 19.65, pillar
height 4.4 mm.
Chain: length 187.5 mm.

Provenance:
Eric Bullivant Bequest, 1974
(WA1974.186)

In 17th-century Geneva there were families which had a
long history of watch-making stretching over genera-
tions. One of those is the Ester family, and this is an
example of the work of Estienne Ester, one of the more
accomplished watchmakers, who lived through most of
the 17th century.

The case of this watch is made from a single piece of
serpentine with gold rims enamelled with flowers and a
twisted ribbon decoration in black, white, red, and yel-
low enamel. Attached to the watch is an associated gold
chain with four turquoise 'buttons' on each link and a
larger piece of amethyst at each end. An engraved bead-
and-reel border on the front-plate surrounds the white
enamel dial, which has a chapter-ring with Roman
hours, diminishing-dot half-hour marks and a quarter-
hour circle. The central area is of white enamel with a
rosette around the central hole. The time is shown by a
single blued-steel hand.

This was the sort of work in which the Geneva
watchmakers excelled. Their productions were diverse
and this may be explained by the fact that in some ways
the apprenticeship system in that city differed from that
practised in other European centres. While, for the most
part, an apprentice in London or Paris would only study
watch-making, in Geneva it was not uncommon for an
apprentice to spend two years learning to be a watchmaker, two years as an engraver, and two years as a lapidary. Estienne Ester himself at the age of twelve went
for two years to the master engraver Estienne Arlaud,
before moving to the watchmaker Jean Baptiste Duboule
(see no. 10).

17. François Rabby

Gold and leather cased verge watch with alarm

Paris, c.1690

Signed: Rabby à Paris

Case: 55.75 mm, thickness
37.3 mm.
Movement: diameter 39.35 mm,
pillar height 10.7 mm.

Provenance:
Eric Bullivant Bequest, 1974
(WA1974.225)

In France, towards the end of the 17th century, a new style of watch appeared which today is called the *oignon* because of its shape and size. These watches were much thicker than their English and Dutch counterparts and they were also different in having a dial on which were separate enamel plaques for each of the hours and a separate enamel ring for the quarter-hours.

The case of this watch is made from brass covered with black leather and with gilt-brass rims and gold piqué-point decoration on the bezel band and back. The alarm is set by turning the hand in the middle of the dial, and the time is shown by a pointer on the disc as it rotates once in twelve hours. When the alarm sounds, a hammer strikes a bell in the back of the case, but here there is no piercing to allow the sound of the bell to escape. Instead, the inner raised gilt-brass rim inside the case is pierced and engraved with foliate scrolls and grotesques.

The watch is wound by using a key on the square in the middle of the dial. Turning the square winds the going train and the alarm at the same time. The finely-made movement has a fusee and is controlled by a large balance wheel beneath a silver bridge pierced and engraved with foliate scrolls and a grotesque mask. The watch has a balance spring, and the rate of the watch is adjusted by turning a square on a geared regulator with a silver index disc engraved 1–7, which alters the effective length of the balance spring to make the watch run more quickly or more slowly.

18. Daniel Le Count

Gold cased verge watch

London, *c.*1680

Signed: Daniel Le Count London

Case: diameter 52.8 mm, thickness 29.0 mm

Movement: diameter 38.25, pillar height 9.4 mm

Provenance:
Formerly in the Albert Schloss Collection, Sold Christie's, London, 16 April 1920, lot 76.
Dyson Perrins Collection (1943)
J. Francis Mallett Bequest, 1947 (WA1947.191.84)

Literature:
F. J. Britten, *Old Clocks and Watches and their Makers*, 5th edn. pp. 200, 217.

During the latter years of the 17th century the question of allegiance to the monarchy was one which arose particularly in relation to the large numbers of French immigrants who were living and working in London at the time. This gave rise to a group of watches with royal emblems which can be seen as expressions of allegiance rather than as watches which actually belonged to any person of royal rank, let alone the king himself. A number of examples exist and, interestingly, nearly all of them were made by Huguenot makers.

This watch by Daniel Le Count is just such a piece, with a gold case cast and chased with floral scrolls. The back has a right-facing profile of Charles II below a royal crown and flanked by lion and unicorn supporters. On the inside, the case is punched with the case maker's mark, TH conjoined, perhaps the mark of Thomas Howe. The gold champlevé dial has minutes numbered 5–60 and hours I–XII around an inner quarter-hour circle which has arrow-head, line, and dot quarter marks around a matted central area. Finely-made blued-steel hands indicate the hours and minutes.

The verge movement is of standard design with fusee and verge escapement and four stylized scroll-top tulip pillars. The steel three-arm balance has the newly-invented spiral steel balance spring of only 1½ turns. This spring has a long straight outer end passing through a curb on a Barrow regulator with a scale numbered 1–5 engraved on the back plate. A key operated micrometer screw adjusts the position of the curb. The pierced and engraved foliate balance cock has a table pierced into three sections and there are small streamers at the sides.

19. Thomas Tompion

Gold cased verge watch
London, 1683
Signed: T Tompion London

Case: diameter 41.3 mm, thickness 24.65 mm.
Movement: diameter 34.6 mm, pillar height 7.95 mm.

Provenance:
J. Francis Mallett Bequest, 1947
(WA1947.191.86)

Literature:
J. F. Hayward, 'Two English Watches in Livrustkammaren', Livrustkammaren, *Journal of the Royal Armoury*, Vol. V., no. 12, p.238
Jeremy Evans, 'The Numbering of Tompion's Watches Series and System', *Antiquarian Horology*, 14 (June 1984), p.588.
David Thompson, 'Watches in the Ashmolean Museum', *Antiquarian Horology*, 25 (Dec 2000), p.625.

Only a very small number of watches are known which bear the signature of the person who engraved the case and this one, signed and dated, *Martin 1683*, is one of them. It is decorated on the back with foliate scrolls incorporating a lion, an eagle, a hound, a monkey, and a serpent, all within a border of figure-of-eight scrolls. The band is engraved with foliage with reclining nude figures and birds and the glazed bezel on the front is engraved with gadroon decoration. The signature *Martin* on the case of this watch is that of Abraham Martin, an engraver from Geneva who was made a Free Brother in the Clockmakers' Company in 1682. While Martin decorated the case, he was not responsible for making its fabric. On the inside is the case-maker's punched mark, ND conjoined beneath a crown, the mark of Nathaniel Delander. Next to that mark are the London hallmarks for 1683 and the number 6 between four dots, Tompion's code for number 406.

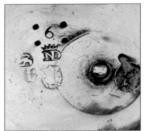

Equally fine in quality to the case is the gold champlevé dial with a chapter-ring with hours numbered I–XII and minutes 5–60 with lozenge half-hour marks around a half-hours circle. The separate central disc is finely engraved with a classical subject with two figures each holding foliage. The time is shown by finely cut bluedsteel hands.

This gilded movement with fusee and verge escapement displays the typical high quality for which Tompion gained a reputation second to none. The tulippattern pillars were commonly used by many of the London makers of the time, demonstrated by those on the preceding watch, by Daniel Le Count (no. 18).

20. Richard Colston

Silver pair-cased verge watch with sun-and-moon dial

London, *c.* 1685–90

Signed: Ri: Colston London 973

Outer Case: diameter 54.2 mm, thickness 28.0 mm
Case: diameter 46.6 mm, thickness 31.2 mm.
Movement: diameter 37.2 mm, pillar height 10.1mm.

Provenance:
Eric Bullivant Bequest, 1974
(WA1974.116)

In London at the end of the 17th century a fashion for unusual dials came into being. One form which was popular was the 'sun-and-moon dial'. Here, the silver champlevé dial has a minute circle numbered 5–60 around the outside, and above the centre there is an aperture numbered VI–XII–VI around the outside with half-hour marks around the inside edge. Beneath the aperture is a rotating blued-steel disc with a gilded sun effigy and an inlaid silver moon and stars, some of which are gilded. There are also crudely scratched clouds which were probably added later. Below the centre two cartouches are inscribed COLSTON and LONDON against a matted ground. The gold minute hand is not original

The plain silver inner case has a winding hole in the back and on the inside is the punched maker's mark SB, the mark of Samuel Bowtell, and the number 973. The outer case is made from brass covered with tortoise-shell, with silver rims and a silver inlaid-wire townscape on the

back. Tortoise-shell became a popular material for all sorts of items from furniture to watch cases in the last quarter of the 17th century. In reality, the material is marine turtle-shell rather than tortoise. Various types were commonly used but principally the hawksbill turtle. By the end of the century cases such as this one, inlaid with wire pictorial decoration, were made in workshops which specialised in working with tortoise-shell, horn, fish-skin (shagreen), and leather.

21. Daniel Quare

Gold pair-cased verge watch with quarter repeat
London, 1687, or shortly after
Signed: D Quare London 611

Dimensions:
Outer case: diameter 54.2 mm,
overall thickness 32.3 mm
Inner case: diameter 47.2 mm,
thickness 30.9 mm
Movement: diameter 36.2 mm,
pillar height 7.5 mm.

Provenance:
Owned by John Stanton of
Benwell, Newcastle (1823).
Charles Dyson Perrins Collection
J. Francis Mallett Bequest, 1947
(WA1947.191.85)

Literature:

In the history of horology there are a small number of
important surviving pieces which mark new advances in
technology, and this watch is one of them. It is by the
celebrated maker, Daniel Quare of London, and is numbered 611. Following Edward Barlow's invention of the
rack striking mechanism for clocks and his subsequent
commissioning of Thomas Tompion to make a repeating
watch in 1687 to secure a patent for his invention,
Daniel Quare claimed that he too had been thinking of
such a device for some time but had never put his
thoughts into practice. He therefore set about making

E. Wood, *Curiosities of Clocks and Watches*, London 1866.

David Thompson, 'Watches in the Ashmolean Museum', *Antiquarian Horology*, 25 (Dec 2000), pp.622–5.

just such a watch which he submitted to the Privy Council on 2 March 1687 in competition with Tompion. William Derham gives an account of the applications to King James II in *Horological Dialogues*, published in 1696 as follows:

> The King, upon tryal of each of them, was pleased to give the preference to Mr Quare's: of which, notice was given soon after in the Gazette. The difference between these two Inventions was, Mr Barlow's was made to Repeat by pushing in two pieces on each side of the Watch-box: one of which Repeated the Hour, the other the Quarter. Mr Quare's was made to Repeat, by a Pin that stuck out near the Pendant which being thrust in (as now 'tis done by thrusting in the Pendant) did repeat both the Hour, and Quarter, with the same thrust.

The allusions on the watch to King James in the inscriptions and in the iconography suggest that this is very likely to be Quare's 1687 watch made for the king or, if not, then certainly one which was commissioned by him very soon afterwards. When looking at the dial with XII at the top, the watch appears to be strangely oriented. A more detailed inspection makes the situation a little clearer, showing that the original concept was for a watch with a pendant at XII and a separate push piece for the repeat at about one o'clock. A restorer at a later date has attached the pendant to the repeat plunger and left the pendant stem as a cut-off stud with no purpose. Now, when the watch is viewed with the pendant up, the XII numeral is not at the top. The dial centre, pierced and engraved with James II's cypher 'RJ JR' surmounted by a royal crown, lies above a blued-steel disc which enhances the appearance of the piercing.

The gold case is finely pierced and engraved, the area on the back with an allegorical scene depicting three bishops beneath a figure of *Justice*, and with the lion and

lamb (symbolizing peace) in the foreground. *Justice* points with a sceptre toward the bishops who have an altar before them. To one side of the altar a group of men appear to be taking bags of money to the Tower of London. To the other side of the altar a similar group also carry bags, with the City of London in the background. Around the outside is a Latin inscription *J.R. 2 . Gloria Deo in excelsis . sine pretio redimimini . Mala lege ablatum . Bono Rege restituitur* (King James II. Glory to God in the highest. You are redeemed without ransom. What was removed by a bad law is restored by a good King).

There is nothing about the movement which makes it stand apart from others of the period or which would preclude it from dating from 1687. The fusee movement with verge escapement has gilt-brass plates with three tulip and two baluster pillars. The repeating work under the dial, however, is of particular importance. It is essentially simple with the quarter snail mounted on a cannon pinion and the hour snail mounted separately on a star wheel. The hammers are operated by a circular rack for

the hours and a shaped rack for the quarters. The mechanism is driven by a small gilt-brass fixed barrel with engraved decoration on the visible side.

There is also a gold outer case which is of interest in that it is not of the same period as the rest of the watch but is nevertheless closely associated with it. This case is engraved with an allegorical scene in which a boat approaches a fortified mole, with *Fame* and two *putti* bearing a royal crown flanking an oval portrait of James II; smaller panels around the band contain royal and military trophies. The case is of 18th-century date, perhaps about 1740, but was clearly made especially for the watch. While there is no proof that this is Quare's actual watch submitted in support of the patent in 1687, there is no doubt that it was made expressly for King James. It is perhaps more likely that it was presented to King James by Quare, a Quaker himself, and given in gratitude to the King for extending religious toleration to the Quakers. King James, following his accession to the throne in 1685, had been instrumental in this change of policy towards Quakers and had also granted the release from prison of a large number of Quakers in 1686. An interesting insight into Quare's religious activities, researched by Bridget Allen, can be found in the 1909 publication *Friends' Quarterly Examiner A Religious, Social & Miscellaneous Review*, No. 133, First month 1909.

22. John Ellicott

Gold pair-cased verge watch with date indicator
London, 1728
Signed: Jnº Ellicott LONDON 1016

Outer case: diameter 49.5 mm,
thickness 22.5 mm.
Inner case: diameter 42.1 mm,
thickness 22.6 mm.
Movement: diameter 32.95 mm,
pillar height 7.98 mm.
Chatelaine: length 117.5 mm,
width 36.8 mm.

Provenance:
Formerly in the Webster
Collection.
J. Francis Mallett Bequest, 1947
(WA1947.191.89)

Literature:
Richard Edgcumbe, *The Art of the
Gold Chaser*, Oxford, 2000, p.58.
David Thompson, 'Watches in the
Ashmolean Museum', *Antiquarian
Horology*, 23 (1997), pp.306–21,
and pp.429–42.

An Ellicott watch would have been a prized possession in the 18th century, and one such as this with triple cases could easily have cost as much as 50 guineas when new. The watch with its *en-suite* chatelaine was attached to the wearer's waist belt by a large hook covered at the front by a *repoussé* design usually in gold but also sometimes in gilded brass. Here a large top hanger with belt hook at the back is attached to three square pierced and engraved foliate plates flanked by a chain of small plates, each embossed with a cherub's head. There are hooks at the sides, one with a red-gold cranked winding key, the other vacant. The plates are decorated with a depiction of *Cephalus and Procris* and three panels showing *Cupid presenting a heart to a lady*.

The plain gold inner case is punched with the London hallmarks for 1728, the case maker's mark IB for John Beasley and the number 1016. The outer *repoussé* case is beautifully chased with a depiction of *Antony and Cleopatra*, the design possibly by Augustin Heckel.

The watch is attached to a gilt-brass chatelaine with a large belt-hook. At the sides are hooks, one with a red-gold, cranked winding key and the other vacant. The plates are decorated with depictions of *Cephalus and Procris* and *Cupid presenting a heart to a lady*.

The dial is typical of the champlevé style with minutes 5–60, hours I–XII and ringed double lozenge half-hour marks around an inner circle divided to half-hours. The central disc is inscribed ELLICOTT and LONDON. A small square aperture above VI o'clock reveals the date on a revolving disc below. There are blued-steel beetle and poker hands.

23. Andreas Grundler

Silver cased quarter-striking, quarter-repeating coach-watch with alarm and date indicator
Friedberg, *c.*1730
Signed: Andreas Grundler Fridtberg

Case: diameter 112.4 mm, thickness 61.0 mm.
Movement: diameter 77.2 mm, pillar height 19.2 mm.

Provenance:
Bentinck Hawkins Bequest 1894, (WA1949.127)

Literature:
Lukas Stolberg, *Die Kutschenuhr*, Munich, 1993, p.35.
David Thompson, 'Watches in the Ashmolean Museum', *Antiquarian Horology*, 25 (Dec 2000), pp. 628–30.

These giant watches, now called coach-watches, were the equivalent of today's travelling alarm clock and were made in relatively small numbers from the 16th century onwards. This example by Andreas Grundler has everything a traveller needed. It is a quarter-striking clockwatch with the option of repeating the strike by depressing the pendant. It also has an alarm and calendar.

To set the alarm, the setting-disc in the dial centre is rotated by applying a key to the small square between x and xi on the half-hour circle. To the left, next to the 45 minute numeral, is a strike/silent lever and, to further add to the sophistication of the watch, there are two small apertures in the dial, one within the iii o'clock numeral which shows the date and a second at the top of the vi o'clock numeral which shows the month. While the minute hand might be original, the hour hand is not.

The silver *repoussé* case has engraved panels of foliage alternating with solid panels decorated with birds, a fox, a pig roasting over a fire, a heron, and a swan. Pierced panels between four solid cartouches depict seated figures, a woman holding a bunch of flowers, one waving with a dog on her lap, a man pouring liquid from a jug into a cup, and another playing a horn. The back of the case has a well-executed depiction of an architectural garden scene with a seated lady and her attendant servants. Also in the design is an engraved shield of arms and crest; the latter, in the form of a heron holding a horse-shoe, can be seen to the right of the seated lady's left hand. These arms and crest have been identified as a variant form of those of the Courtoys family of Lincoln.

24. Strigner (Jakob Strixner)

Gold and stone-set mother-of-pearl pair-cased quarter-repeating verge watch with *en-suite* chatelaine.

Friedberg, *c.*1740

Signed: Strigner Lond 48

Outer case: diameter 47.8 mm, thickness 26.5 mm.
Inner case: diameter 41.0 mm, thickness 28.7 mm.
Movement: diameter 30.4 mm, pillar height 7.19 mm.
Chatelaine: length 126.0 mm, width 29.4 mm.

Provenance:
Eric Bullivant Bequest, 1974
(WA1974.166)

Literature:
David Thompson, 'Watches in the Ashmolean Museum', *Antiquarian Horology*, 25 (Dec 2000), pp.630–1.

This pair cased verge watch with *en-suite* chatelaine has an intriguing background. Although signed *Strigner Lond 48* there is nothing about the design of the movement to suggest a London origin and there are no references to a maker with the name Strigner in London in the 1740s. However, there was a family of watchmakers in Friedberg called Strixner and Jakob Strixner, who lived between 1699 and 1770, is probably the maker of this watch.

A very similar example of this type of case exists on a watch signed *Renpuarg London no 4*. The spelling of the name Graupner in reverse may be significant in identifying the origin as South Germany. While there is no evidence of a Graupner in London, there was a family of watchmakers by that name in Augsburg in the first half of the 18th century. Friedberg is only a short distance

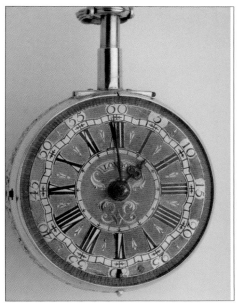

from Augsburg and it is likely that Augsburg case makers worked for Friedberg watchmakers. The close similarity of the two watch cases points to a common origin for them and that, in turn, leads to the conclusion that both the Strigner and 'Renpuarg' watches have a Friedberg/Augsburg origin.

The gilt-brass inner case is pierced and engraved with foliate scrolls, strap-work, birds, and animals and the middle of the back is decorated with musical instruments. The gold outer case has alternating pierced and solid panels set with mother-of-pearl inlaid with a gold cartouche which itself is set with a garnet. There are also pierced and solid panels decorated with a male bust, a basket of flowers and a female bust. Both cases are punched on the inside with the case-maker's mark 'AG' probably that of Antoni Grill III. The *en-suite* chatelaine has two hooks, one carrying a winding key and seal, the other with an intaglio classical bust.

25. George Graham

Gold pair-cased cylinder watch with quarter repeat
London, 1744
Signed: G. Graham London 826

Outer case: diameter 48.3 mm,
thickness 22.0 mm.
Inner case: diameter 41.0 mm,
thickness 27.1 mm.
Movement: diameter 29.4 mm,
pillar height 5.7 mm.

Provenance:
Julius Rosenberger Collection,
sold Sotheby's, London, 1943.
Eric Bullivant Bequest, 1974
(WA1974.132)

Literature:
Richard Edgcumbe, *The Art of the
Gold Chaser in Eighteenth-Century
London*, Oxford, 2000, p.102,
fig.83.
David Thompson, 'Watches in the
Ashmolean Museum', *Antiquarian
Horology*, 25 (Sept 2000),
pp.626–8.

Exhibition:
Rococo, Victoria and Albert
Museum, 1984 p. 131, no. H9.

In the 1740s, the combination of a George Graham cylinder watch with quarter-repeat together with fine gold cases, the outer *repoussé* case decorated by George Michael Moser, was the height of fashion and such a watch might also have had an *en-suite* gold *repoussé* chatelaine.

Two features in this watch are significant. Firstly, the watch has a cylinder escapement, a technical improvement in watches introduced by George Graham in about 1726. The new escapement was based on an earlier idea of Thomas Tompion's in 1695, and such faith did Graham have in his new invention that thenceforth he used it exclusively. George Graham was also one of the first makers to use the white enamel dial from about 1725, a new more visible style which replaced the earlier champlevé dials.

The gold pair cases are both marked with the maker's mark *JW* for John Ward and the inner case is hallmarked London 1744. The outer case has a chased *repoussé* depiction of a classical wedding with Juno in the background. The chaser's signature *G.Moser:fec* appears on a small reserve below the scene. Richard Edgcumbe in *The Art of the Gold Chaser* notes that the depiction appears on a number of other watches and in the Victoria and Albert Museum there is a Moser drawing of it, suggesting that it is probably his own design.

The watch also has a quarter repeat mechanism with a small pulse-piece between v and vi which, when pressed in, allows the operator to feel the hours and quarters as a pulse in the button but prevents the hammers from striking the bell, thus providing the time to the owner without making too much disturbing sound.

26. Ferdinand Berthoud

Gold and enamel cased verge watch with quarter repeat

Paris, 1769

Signed: Ferdinand Berthoud à Paris No.427.

Case: diameter 40.1 mm, thickness 19.3 mm.
Movement: diameter 37.4 mm, pillar height 10.0 mm.

Provenance:
J. Francis Mallett Bequest
(WA1947.191.116)

Literature:
David Thompson, 'Watches in the Ashmolean Museum', *Antiquarian Horology*, 25 (Dec 2000), pp.632–3.

Swiss-born Ferdinand Berthoud was one of the most renowned Parisian clock and watchmakers of the 18th century. In contrast to some of his pioneering pieces, however, this watch is of standard form. The movement is a design commonly made in Paris during this period. It has gilded plates and four tapered pillars. There is a fusee with chain which drives a four-wheel gear train which terminates with a verge escapement controlled by a brass three-arm balance and spiral balance spring. The geared regulator has a silver index disc engraved 'AVANCE' and 'RETARD' for adjusting the rate of the watch.

A 'dumb' quarter-repeat mechanism taps the last hour and quarter on the case when the pendant is pressed in. To adjust the speed of striking there is a variable-depth plug-bearing for the last pinion in the gear train. The back plate is engraved with a scale marked 'V' and 'L' for *vite* and *lentement* to indicate which way to turn the plug.

The white enamel dial is supported by a gilt-brass dial-plate signed *Ferdinand Berthoud* around the edge. The dial itself is typical of French dials of this period with bold minute and hour numerals around an inner single-line circle. It is signed *Ferdinand Berthoud* above and below the centre. The minute hand is an un-gilded brass replacement but the hour hand appears to be original.

The three-colour gold case has a bezel and band decorated with a figure-of-eight wreath design in relief. The back has a wreath border enclosing a painted enamel panel in sepia tones depicting *Cupid* drawing his bow. There is also a pulse-piece at vii–viii for silent repeat. On the inside, the case is punched with the Paris hallmarks for 1769 in the form of a floral purity mark and a crowned letter F date mark. The mark JAA with a cinquefoil above is that of Jean-Antoine Alazard.

27. Thomas Mudge & William Dutton

Gold and enamel pair-cased cylinder watch with quarter striking and half-quarter repeat
London, *c.*1773
Signed: Tho. Mudge W. Dutton London 982.

Outer case: diameter 58.4 mm, thickness 23.2 mm.
Inner case: diameter 50.1 mm, thickness 29.5 mm.
Movement: diameter 37.5 mm, pillar height 6.15 mm.
Overall thickness 30.0 mm.

Provenance:
Made for John Montagu, 4th Earl of Sandwich.
Eric Bullivant Bequest, (WA1974.153)

Literature:
David Thompson, 'Watches in the Ashmolean Museum', *Antiquarian Horology*, 25 (Dec 2000), pp.634, 635.

This repeating clock-watch by Thomas Mudge and William Dutton is of the high quality associated with one of England's celebrated watch-making partnerships. It has a fusee and a cylinder escapement. Under the dial is a rack striking mechanism for hours and quarters, the hour snail with twelve lobes each with three steps. The pendant-operated half-quarter repeat mechanism is of Matthew Stogden's design and both it and the quarter striking use a single bell in the back of the case. In the case band, there is a pulse-piece which, when held down, allows the repeat to operate without striking the bell. The name 'Drury' is scratched on the back of the bell.

The gold inner case is pierced and engraved with panels of foliate scrolls with a grotesque mask at the bottom and a harbour scene around the pendant foot. The inside

is punched with the maker's mark PM, the mark of Peter
Mounier. The gold and enamel outer case is enamelled
en -basse-taille in blue and white around the bezel and
band. On the back is a ribbon border, tied in a knot at
the top and entwined with floral sprays and palm fronds
at the bottom. This encloses a central medallion of blue
guilloché enamel with a left-facing griffin's head crowned
with a red and white earl's coronet on a blue and white
torse, the crest of the Earls of Sandwich. This case is also
punched PM on the inside. The watch is likely to have
been owned by John, 4th Earl of Sandwich, statesman,
diplomat, Secretary of State, and First Lord of the
Admiralty (1718–92). The harbour scene engraved
around the pendant foot was probably specially commissioned to give the watch a nautical flavour. John
Montagu is also famous for inventing the concept of the
sandwich as an easy way to eat bread and meat while
gambling.

28. William Ilbery

Gold and enamel cased duplex watch for the Chinese market

London and Fleurier, Switzerland, *c.*1810

Signed: Ilbery London 6582.

From the third quarter of the 18th century onwards, England had a flourishing export trade in clocks and watches to China via the East India Company through Canton. One English maker who specialized in this trade was William Ilbery but this watch exposes him as a maker not supporting the English economy. As well as his business in London he had connections with Fleurier in Switzerland, and this watch has all the characteristics of one made there. Ilbery's role in its export to China was probably no more than retailer. Indeed, it would come as no surprise to find the name of one of the makers, Bovet or Juvet engraved on this watch, so typical is it of Fleurier work for the Chinese market.

The gold and enamel case is enamelled with green vine leaves and raised seed-pearl white grapes over a black ground. The centre of the back is an enamelled still life of flowers and fruit on a translucent red ground. The gold pendant is enamelled in black, the oval top and bow set with split pearls. A push-piece in the pendant releases the sprung back. On the inside a steel pin at the side releases a sprung and hinged inner dome, enamelled with a border of flowers around a lozenge pattern, each light blue enamel lozenge decorated with a gold quatrefoil at its centre.

The whole of the movement is engraved with foliate scrolls and the mainspring barrel has typical 'Chinese' geared stop-work recessed into the barrel cover. The balance and spring are regulated by an index on the balance cock table, registering against an engraved scale.

Case: diameter 60.0mm, thickness 20.9mm.
Movement: diameter 49.8mm.

Provenance:
Price Collection 1928,
(WA1949.112)

For a detailed history of the Swiss export of watches to China and the watchmakers who specialized in that market see Alfred Chapuis, *La Montre Chinoise*, Neuchâtel, nd., particularly pp.180–4 on William Ilbery.

Literature:
David Thompson, 'Watches in the Ashmolean Museum', *Antiquarian Horology*, 25 (Dec 2000), pp.636–8.

29. Breguet et Fils

Gold cased cylinder watch *montre à tact*
Paris, *c.*1820
Signed: Breguet HORGER DE LA MARINE N.3495

Case: diameter 39.5mm, thickness 8.1mm.

Provenance:
Eric Bullivant Bequest, 1974 (WA1974.193).

Literature:
David Thompson, 'Watches in the Ashmolean Museum', *Antiquarian Horology*, 25 (Dec 2000), pp.635–6.

One of the most celebrated makers in the history of watch-making is Abraham Louis Breguet, a Swiss émigré who made his fame and fortune in Paris by establishing one of the most accomplished workshops of the time and making watches with a characteristic and identifiable 'Breguet' style.

One particular Breguet design was the *montre à tact* and this example was made in Paris in about 1820. It has a gold engine-turned case with a hinged cover on which there are hour numerals. Mounted in the middle of the cover a robust gold hand with a pierced aperture shows the hour beneath as it is turned and registers with the touch pins around the case band. Turning this hand clockwise will simply allow a stop on the inside to ratchet over the tail of the substantial hour hand below. Turning it anti-clockwise will cause the outside hand to be stopped by the hour hand beneath so that the time could be ascertained by touch on the outside. Consequently these watches would have been useful for those who were blind or who had poor sight. However, it has been suggested that they were equally useful to sighted people in the dark or in circumstances where the owner would not wish to be observed looking at the time.

The case was made by M. A. Buffelard, whose mark 'MAB' with a triangle above is punched inside the back along with Paris hallmarks used between 1819 and 1838. Beneath the *à tact* cover is an engine-turned silver dial with hours I–XII and an outer circle of dots for the minutes. The movement is a small-size Breguet *souscription* calibre with a ruby cylinder escapement and the gold balance and spiral balance spring have Breguet's 'parachute' anti-shock suspension device.

30. Edward Prior

Gold and enamel triple cased verge watch made for the Turkish market, London, c.1820
Signed: Edw. Prior 16766 London

Outer case: diameter 44.3mm, thickness 16.0mm.
Middle case: diameter 38.9mm, thickness 14.5mm.
Inner case: diameter 33.1mm, thickness 19.4mm.
Movement: diameter 26.65mm, pillar height 4.7mm.
Overall thickness 23.85mm.

Provenance:
Eric Bullivant Bequest, 1974
(WA1974.158)

Alongside a flourishing trade in the export of watches to China, there were those who manufactured watches specifically for the export to the Ottoman Empire. They sold their wares through trading outlets in Constantinople and towards the end of the 18th century and into the 19th century, the name of Prior becomes synonymous with that trade, firstly with George Prior and later with Edward.

This charming example, of small size, is typical of the 19th-century 'Turkish-market' watch which commonly had triple cases and in the best instances has gold cases enamelled in colours depicting western European subjects but also sometimes with Middle Eastern decorative elements. Here the scalloped edge to the cases is typical and the subject of the decoration is that of musical instruments with a musical score, the latter being anything but familiar in Islamic culture. The inner case is punched with a London hallmark, the date letter is indistinct, and the punched maker's mark SK in a rectangle is probably that of Samuel Keene.

The dial has numerals commonly found in the 'Turkish market' clocks and watches where makers invented a form of numeral which was in effect a sort of hybrid between the Roman and true Arabic systems. The gold beetle and poker style hands are old-fashioned for 1820.

The movement with verge escapement is equally old-fashioned for the period but here again it seems to have been common practice. The serial number 16766, on the back of the movement, gives an idea of the scale of production involved in watch-making in the early years of the 19th century.

31. E. Dent & Company

Gold hunter-cased pocket chronometer, London, 1869
Signed: 'No. 32405 Dent. Watchmaker to the Queen.
61 Strand and 34 Royal Exchange. London' and DENT.
61 STRAND.LONDON 32403

Case: diameter 51.9mm, thickness
13.7mm.
Movement: diameter 41.0 mm.
Provenance:
Eric Bullivant Bequest, 1974
(WA1974.119)

Literature:
David Thompson, 'Watches in the
Ashmolean Museum', *Antiquarian
Horology,* 25 (Dec 2000), pp.638–9.

This fine gold hunter-cased pocket chronometer by
Edward Dent & Company of London was made in 1869
and is of the highest quality. Apart from the usual subsidiary seconds dial at VI o'clock, the finely enamelled
dial has an 'up-and-down' dial below the XII numeral to
show when the watch needs winding.

The 18 carat gold case is embossed all over with
foliage and in the centre of the back is an enamelled
monogram WPE. On the inside, the case is punched
with London hallmarks, but without a date letter, and
with the case-maker's mark LN in an oval cameo, the
mark of Louis Norbier. The front cover is punched inside
with JWS in cameo for James Walter Stack and the
London date letter for 1869.

The existence of two different marks in the case
might be explained by the bankruptcy of Louis Norbier
in 1867. Perhaps the watch case was incomplete when
Norbier's business closed and was repossessed by Dent,
who then sent it to Stock's workshop to be finished.

The movement is a fine-quality half-plate with an
Earnshaw-type spring-detent escapement with split
bimetallic compensation balance with gold screws
around the rims and a free sprung blued-steel helical balance spring. The inconsistency in the numbering on the
dial case and movement might suggest that the watch
was part of a batch being made at the same time and
where the movement and case were not in the last resort
used together.

Brief Biographies

JOHN BEASLEY, watch case maker, worked at 'The Sun, Holborn Bridge', London, and was described as a 'Free Clockmaker' i.e., a Freeman in the Clockmakers' Company when his mark was registered at Goldsmiths' Hall on 14 March 1720. Beasley was apprenticed to Thomas Nichols, also a watch case maker, in 1709 and gained his Freedom in the Clockmakers' Company in March 1719. He had his business in Dean Street, Fetter Lane, in 1725 and is thought to have died in 1732.

FERDINAND BERTHOUD was born in Plancemont, Switzerland, in 1727. In 1747 he went to Paris and became Master in the Paris Guild in 1754. He was married twice, firstly to a Mlle. Chatri of Caen in 1782 and secondly to Mlle. De Moustier from St. Quentin. He wrote extensively on both the technology and the history of timekeeping. He was *Horloger Pensionnaire du Roi* and also *Inspecteur Général des Machines pour la Marine*. His business was in Rue de Harlay in Paris. He died in 1807.

JAN JANSSEN BOCKELTS the elder. Little is known of this maker, except that he came from Aachen, but is known to have been working in Haarlem by 1607. He died in about 1626.

SAMUEL BOWTELL, London watch case maker, was apprenticed in the Clockmakers' Company in 1674 and became a Freeman in that Company in 1681. He became an Assistant in the Company in 1710 but is thought to have died in that year.

ABRAHAM LOUIS BREGUET was without doubt one of the most ingenious of all watch and clockmakers. He was born in 1747 in Neuchâtel in Switzerland. At the age of

18 he moved to Paris, then to Versailles where he studied with the watch maker Etienne Gide. He married Cécile Lhuillier, in 1775 and established his own business at Quai de L'Horloge in Paris in partnership with Xavier Gide, the brother of his former master. He very quickly rose to eminence, becoming Clockmaker to Louis XVI and was soon supplying watches and clocks to the nobility of Europe. He suffered problems during the French Revolution and spent time in exile in Switzerland, but when France settled down in the Empire of Napoleon Bonaparte he returned and became Clockmaker to the Emperor. Abraham Louis Breguet took his son Louis Antoine into partnership in 1816 and from then the name became Breguet et Fils. Following Abraham Louis' death in 1823, Louis Antoine continued the business which produced some of the finest watches made in the 19th century, the Breguet watch-making business which still exists today.

AUGUSTE BRETTONNEAU is known to have been working in Paris between 1633 and 1643.

RICHARD COLSTON, the son of John Colston, was admitted to the Clockmakers' Company by Patrimony in 1682. He is thought to have died in about 1703.

PIERRE COMBRET was a watchmaker who was born in Egletons but is known to have been working in Lyon from about 1570. He married Benoîte Jourdan in 1591 but she died only two years later. In the following year Combret married Anne Couchaud, the daughter of a Lyon goldsmith, and in the years up to 1616 they had 17 children. His business was in Rue de Flandre 'between the Porcelet and the Exchange'. He died in 1622 and was buried at the church of St Laurent, Lyon, on 26 December 1622.

RICHARD CRAYLE was born about 1600 and was admitted as a member of the Blacksmiths' Company in

London in 1626. His business was in Fleet Street. He was later a petitioner for the founding of the Clockmakers' Company and to that end in 1630 he pledged £5 towards the funds. He retired from active business in 1660 and is thought to have died in 1671.

NATHANIEL DELANDER, watch case maker, became a Free Brother in the Clockmakers' Company in 1669, and Assistant in 1689. He is though to have died in about 1691.

E. J. DENT & COMPANY: founded by Edward John Dent (1790–1853). He studied watch repeat-mechanism making with Richard Rippon and worked as a watch finisher until 1830 when he went into partnership with John Roger Arnold. Following Arnold's death in 1843 he went into business on his own again. He married Richard Rippon's widow and continued the business until his death in 1853, at which time the firm was in the middle of making the great Westminster clock (Big Ben). After Edward's death the firm was carried on by his stepsons, Richard and Frederick. The business continued during the 19th century under the direction of successive members of the Dent and Rippon families.

JEAN BAPTISTE DUBOULE was the second son of the watchmaker Martin Duboule and his wife Suzanne of Geneva. He was baptized on 4 June 1615 in Geneva and died on 6 April 1694.

WILLIAM DUTTON was apprenticed in the Clockmakers' Company to George Graham in 1738 and gained his Freedom in 1746. In about 1755 Dutton went into partnership with Thomas Mudge and continued the business on his own after Mudge's death in 1794.

EDWARD EAST was born in 1602 in the village of Southill in Bedfordshire. In March 1618 he was apprenticed in the London Goldsmiths' Company to Richard Rogers and gained his Freedom in that company in

1627. When the Clockmakers' Company was founded in 1631, he became one of the first Assistants. He later served as Warden in 1638 and twice as Master in 1645 and 1653. His business was at various addresses, firstly in Pall Mall but later in Fleet Street at the sign of the Musical Clock in the 1640s. Towards the end of his life he was at 'The Sun' outside Temple Bar. In 1660 he was appointed Royal Clockmaker to Charles II. He died in 1697 having been the head of a prolific workshop producing clocks and watches for a large part of the 17th century. In 1693 he gave £100 to the Master, Wardens, and Fellowship of the Clockmakers' Company in trust, to pay five Freemen, or their widows, twenty shillings annually by two half-yearly payments.

JOHN ELLICOTT FRS was born in 1703, the son of John Ellicott Senior, a Freeman in the Clockmakers' Company in 1696 who died in 1733. John Ellicott junior was apprenticed in 1719/20 in the Clothworkers' Company to Richard Ward, and gained his freedom in that Company in 1726. He went on to continue running his father's business with great success and was Clockmaker to King George III. The business was at 17 Sweetings Alley, Royal Exchange, London although John Junior lived in Mare Street, Hackney. He died in 1772 and was succeeded in the business by his son Edward Ellicott and thereafter by his grandson, also Edward, who continued the business until it finally closed down in the 1840s.

LEONHARD ENGELSCHALCKH (fl.1650s–1685) was living in Friedberg in the 1650s when he married Anna Gerschlacher on 16 June 1654. Leonhard and Anna had two sons, Johann Christian and Johann Georg, both of whom became clock and watchmakers. Leonhard died in Friedberg in July 1685.

ESTIENNE ESTER, watchmaker of Geneva, was the eldest son of Hans Heinrich Ester. Estienne was born in 1629 and at the age of 12 was sent as an apprentice to

Estienne Arlaud, a master engraver. He stayed there for two years and then, in 1643, went to Jean Baptiste Duboule to train as a watchmaker. In 1649, probably soon after he had finished his apprenticeship, he married Elizabeth Rousseau, the daughter of the watchmaker Jean Rousseau, the great grandfather of Jean-Jacques Rousseau, the 18th-century philosopher. Estienne Ester died in 1707.

ZACHARIE FONNEREAU is known to have been working between 1618 and the mid-1640s. He came originally from Geneva but was in Lyon in 1618 and became a Compagnon in 1622. He later moved to La Rochelle where he became a Master in 1641 and is thought to have died soon afterwards.

GEORGE GRAHAM FRS was born either at Horsegill, Kirklington, or at Fordlands in Irthlington, both in Cumberland, in about 1673. In 1688 he was apprenticed to Henry Aske in the Clockmakers' Company in London and became a Freeman of the Company in 1695, after which he began working for Thomas Tompion. In 1696 he married Tompion's niece Elizabeth and was in partnership with Tompion from 1711 until Tompion's death in 1713 leaving Graham the business in his will. Graham continued to trade at the Dial and Three Crowns in Fleet Street until 1720 when he moved the business across the road to new premises next to the Duke of Marlborough tavern. In 1722, Graham held the office of Master of the Clockmakers' Company. He died in 1751 and was buried in Westminster Abbey with his mentor Thomas Tompion. As well as making clocks and watches Graham was responsible for providing astronomical instruments for the Royal Greenwich Observatory. He became a Fellow of the Royal Society in 1721 and is renowned for his development of the cylinder escapement for watches in about 1726, based on an invention by Tompion, and for his extensive use of the white enamel dial from the mid-1720s.

ABRAHAM GRIBELIN was the son of Simon Gribelin, a watchmaker and engraver of Blois. He was born in 1589 and became established as a watchmaker in his own right in 1614, succeeding his father as Clockmaker to the King. He was the father of fifteen children born between 1620 and 1638 to his wife, née Judith Festeau. He died in 1671.

ANDREAS GRUNDLER was born in Kissing in 1705 and, after becoming a journeyman clockmaker, he applied to become a citizen of Friedberg as he intended to marry the daughter of a Friedberg citizen. His life was short and, judging from the number of marriages, not blessed with good fortune. He married three times in the space of three or four years, most probably because his wives died in childbirth. His first marriage was in 1733 when he was 28 years old. Just two years later he married again and a third time in 1736. He died in December 1740 at the age of only 35.

WILLIAM ILBERY is recorded as working in London from 1780 until his death in 1839. He first had a business in Goswell Road, Clerkenwell and later at 24 York Place, City Road. However, Ilbery and his son also had business operations both in Fleurier in Switzerland and in Canton in China.

SAMUEL KEENE, watch case maker, registered a series of punches at Goldsmiths' Hall between 1802 and 1808.

HANS KOCH worked in Munich in the second half of the 16th century. He became *Hofuhrmacher* to the Elector Albrecht V of Bavaria in 1554, a post which he held until his death in about 1603.

DANIEL LE COUNT, a French Huguenot, lived and worked in London. He became Freeman in the Haberdashers' Company and a Free Brother in the Clockmakers' Company in 1676. He is known to have been working until about 1705.

GEORGE MICHAEL MOSER was born in Schaffhausen, Switzerland, in 1706. He later moved to Geneva, where he became an accomplished goldsmith and enameller. He came to London in 1726 and began working for a coppersmith. Before long he was working for an immigrant German gold-chaser, Johannes Valentine Haidt. At some time in the 1730s, together with Haidt, he established a small drawing class specializing in life classes, to utilize his talent in drawing. In the 1740s Moser became a leading figure at the St Martin's Lane Academy and later, in 1769, he became the first Keeper of the Royal Academy. His *repoussé* watch case work and his pictorial enamels are among the finest ever made. Moser died in 1783.

THOMAS MUDGE (see also William Dutton): Thomas Mudge was born in Plymouth in about 1715, the son of the Reverend Zachariah Mudge. At the age of fourteen in 1730 he was apprenticed to the celebrated maker George Graham. Following his training he married Abigail Hopkins in 1738 and began working in his own right. He became clockmaker to George III in 1776 and was renowned for making complicated pieces for King Ferdinand VI and the Spanish royal court. In 1750 he opened his own shop in Fleet Street. Just a year later in 1751 his old master, George Graham, died and Mudge the very next day advertised his services. *Thomas Mudge, Watchmaker, late Apprentice to Mr. Graham, deceased, carries on Business in the same Manner Mr. Graham did, at the sign of the Dial and one Crown, opposite the Bolt and Ton in Fleet Street.* Mudge went on to become one of the foremost makers of clocks, watches, and chronometers, developing the gravity escapement for regulators and constant-force escapements for chronometers. In about 1748 he completed his experimental clock, incorporating his newly invented detached lever escapement, which in a developed form was to become standard for everyday watches in the 19th and 20th centuries.

FRANCIS NAWE or Nau was born in Brabant but in 1583, in the census *Returns of the Aliens*, he is recorded as a member of the Dutch Church in Austin Friars, London. Nawe's time in London was short as he died in 1593.

NICOLE AND NORBIER: The watch case making partnership of Alexis Nicole and Louis Norbier was dissolved in 1865. After continuing in business on his own, Louis Norbier of 7 Meredith Street, Clerkenwell was declared bankrupt in 1867. However, by 1869 he seems to have recovered his business and was working at 146 Cheapside. Later, in 1875, he was at 31 Northampton Square, Clerkenwell.

EDWARD PRIOR is known to have been working at 18 Powell Street in Clerkenwell, London, from the early 19th century until 1870.

DANIEL QUARE, a London maker was born in about 1649. He was a Quaker who became a Free Brother in the Clockmakers' Company in London in 1671 and rose to the offices of Assistant in 1700, Warden in 1705, and Master in 1708. In about 1716 he went into partnership with Stephen Horseman. He died in 1724 and was buried in the Quakers' burial ground at Bunhill Fields. From that time the business was continued by Horseman although the business name remained the same, until bankruptcy befell him in 1733.

FRANÇOIS RABBY was married in 1686 to the niece of Corneille Godefroy. He worked in Rue de Harlay, Paris, from 1698 and later in Place Dauphine. In 1718 he was imprisoned for marrying one of his daughters to a Genevan Protestant at the English ambassador's house.

DAVID RAMSAY was born in Scotland. When James I succeeded to the throne of England in 1603 he sent for David Ramsay, who was at that time living in France, probably in Blois. On his return Ramsay was appointed

Page of the Bedchamber, Groom of the Privy Chamber, and Keeper of all his Majesty's Clocks and Watches. Later, in 1613, he was appointed Clockmaker Extraordinary, with a pension of £50 per year. In November 1618 he was made Chief Clockmaker and finally in July 1619 letters of Denization were granted to him, allowing him English citizenship. In 1632 Ramsay was appointed first Master of the newly founded Worshipful Company of Clockmakers. His appearances at Court meetings, however, appear to have been infrequent, the Court being mostly presided over by Henry Archer, the Deputy Master, for the first year of the Company's existence.

JAMES WALTER STOCK was a watch case maker of 19 Green Terrace, New River Head, Clerkenwell.

JAKOB STRIXNER was born in 1699 and married Maria Sacker in 1725 and later Cecile (whose surname is unknown) in 1743. He is recorded at house number 81 in Friedberg in 1740. There were three sons, Franz, Andreas, and Johann Jacob.

THOMAS TOMPION was baptized on 25 July 1639 in the parish church of Northill in Bedfordshire and lived in the nearby hamlet of Ickwell Green. Nothing is known of his early career or where he learned the art of clock- and watch-making. However, in 1671, at the age of 32, he can be traced in London where he had established a business in Water Lane just off Fleet Street and where he rapidly rose to eminence. In 1674, he supplied a turret clock for the Wardrobe Tower at the Tower of London and a quadrant for the Royal Society, and the following year he made a watch for King Charles II. In 1675–6 he was commissioned to make the regulators for the new Greenwich Royal Observatory. In the years that followed, Tompion went on to become the most celebrated of all English clockmakers and established a business with a reputation second to none in Europe. He was admitted as a Free Brother in the Clockmakers' Company in 1671, was granted full freedom in 1674 and held the office of Master of the Company in 1703/4. He died in 1713 and was buried in Westminster Abbey.

JOHN WARD, a watch case maker, was apprenticed to William Sherwood, a master who made cases for both Thomas Tompion and George Graham. Ward became Free in the Clockmakers' Company in July 1730.

Note: *The information in the above biographies was gleaned from numerous sources mentioned in the bibliography. Readers are encouraged to consult the various works for more detailed information.*

Glossary

Aspectarium

A diagram designed to show the aspect or angular relationship between celestial bodies, particularly the sun, moon, and earth. The most common aspects are opposition (180°) shown as an infinity sign, trine (120°) a triangle, and quartile (90°) shown as a square.

Balance cock

The component on the back of a watch movement with a foot attached to the movement and a raised table in which there is a small hole for the balance pivot. The cock in early watches fits over a rectangular stud and is secured by a transverse pin. In later watches, the cock is attached to the movement plate by a screw.

Balance

The oscillating part in a watch which controls the rate at which the device will run and consequently determines the accuracy of its timekeeping. Before the introduction of the balance spring in 1675, the balance, like the dumb-bell balance had no natural period of oscillation and consequently, its timekeeping ability was affected by changes in impulse given by the escapement to keep it swinging. The performance of the balance was greatly improved in 1657 by the introduction of the spiral balance spring.

Balance, dumb-bell

The dumb-bell balance is associated with watches made in 16th-century Germany. It consists of a small weighted bar which looks like a miniature dumb-bell and provides the timekeeping element in the watch. Like the balance, the dumb-bell has no natural period of oscillation and so will swing faster or slower depending on the amount of impulse given to it by the escape wheel (see escapement). In the more sophisticated versions, the small disc-shaped weight at each end of the bar is adjustable to allow for fine regulation, although like the foliotcontrolled clock, accuracy of better than half an hour per day could not be expected.

Balance spring
An important innovation developed by Robert Hooke in London and Christiaan Huygens in the Netherlands which made the oscillating balance isochronous – taking the same time to swing through large or small arcs. This momentous invention greatly improved the timekeeping properties of the watch, reducing the error from as much as twenty minutes a day to less than one minute per day in a good-quality watch.

Escapement
The part of a watch which connects the train of wheels to the balance. It has two functions; to transfer energy to the balance to keep it in motion and to allow the escape wheel only to rotate tooth by tooth so that the motion of the balance controls the timekeeping of the watch. Many escapement mechanisms have been invented, but the most common were the *verge*, the *cylinder*, the *detached lever* and the *spring-detent*.

Escapement, cylinder
Invented by George Graham in about 1726, based on earlier work by Thomas Tompion, this escapement improved accuracy in watches. Instead of the crown wheel and verge of the verge escapement a slotted hollow cylinder was used to impart impulse to the balance and lock and unlock the escape wheel. Because the cylinder is circular, when the escape wheel tooth is locked by the cylinder it causes no movement in the escape wheel, thus reducing the interference with the balance during its supplementary arc.

Escapement, detached lever
Invented by Thomas Mudge in about 1754 and developed to become the most commonly used escapement for mechanical watches from the middle of the 19th century until today. A lever placed between the escape wheel and the oscillating balance has two pallets which alternately lock the escape wheel teeth. Most of the time the lever is staionary in one of two positions, but during a small part of each swing, the balance moves the lever to the other position, allowing a tooth to pass

and at the same time receiving an impulse. This intermittent action aids timekeeping by 'detaching' the balance from the escapement and the gear wheels for a large part of its arc of swing.

Escapement, spring-detent

Patented in 1782 by John Arnold and 1783 by Thomas Wright for Thomas Earnshaw, this escapement employs a steel detent, partly made as a spring. The detent carries a locking stone and a passing spring which act with the teeth of the escape wheel in locking and unlocking and with the jewelled rollers on the balance arbor for unlocking and giving impulse. The major advantage of this escapement, developed primarily for use in marine chronometers, was that it needed no oil on its acting surfaces.

Escapement, verge

The origins of the verge escapement remain obscure but it was known in clockwork from as early as the 15th century. In watches the escapement consists of an escape wheel, commonly called the crown wheel, and two pallets on an axle or arbor, known as the verge, to which the balance is attached. The oscillating action of the balance causes the pallets to swing through an arc, allowing alternate teeth of the escape wheel to be released and locked on each swing of the balance.

Fusee

A device invented some time during the 15th century which is used to even out the unequal force produced by a mainspring as it unwinds. The fusee is on the same arbor as the great wheel, and has the shape of a truncated curved cone with a spiral groove on it. A line or chain, wound around the spring barrel, has one end fastened to the fusee at its largest radius. When the fusee is turned to wind the clock, the line is pulled off the barrel onto the groove on the fusee, turning the barrel and winding the spring. When the line has been wound onto the whole spiral groove, the spring is fully wound, and the line pulls on the smallest radius of the fusee where its mechanical advantage is least. The fusee turns the gear train and, as the clock runs, the spring pulls the line off the fusee and back onto the barrel, but acting on an ever-increasing radius of the fusee thanks to its conical shape. The increasing radius increases the mechanical advantage, compensating for the reducing force of the spring as it unwinds, until at the end of the run, when the force of the spring is at its least, the line is pulling on the largest radius of the fusee.

Going barrel

A mainspring barrel in a clock or watch in which the great wheel is mounted on the barrel itself and the mainspring is wound from the centre and produces torque in the direction of motion of the going train. A ratchet system prevents the mainspring from unwinding in the wrong direction.

Going Train

The wheels and pinions in a watch which transmit motion from the driving force, the mainspring, to the escapement. In most watches these usually consist of four wheels and three pinions; great wheel, centre wheel (which rotates once per hour and carries the minute hand), third wheel, and fourth wheel (in watches arranged to rotate once per minute to carry a seconds hand).

Maintaining power

A mechanism incorporated in a watch designed to keep it running whilst it is being wound up. Originally designed for use in clocks, the principles were developed in the 18th century by John Harrison for use in portable timekeepers and his spring-powered device, commonly called 'Harrison's maintaining power', is the one normally found in better quality watches. In this device a spring powered ratchet situated in the great-wheel and fusee assembly continues to exert a force on the great wheel when the machine is being wound. This system was adopted for more sophisticated portable clocks such as marine chronometers and was extensively used in watches in the 19th century.

Pair-cased watch

A watch in which the movement is housed in an inner case which itself is then contained was a second, outer, case. In earlier centuries the inner case was often referred to as the box and the outer case as the case or pair-case.

Repeating watch
A watch designed to indicate the hours and the quarters or
even the hours, quarters, and minutes by striking a bell or
gong(s) or by tapping a block inside the watch case – a dumb
repeater. In the 19th century such watches were called 'Tattlers'
in the sense of being tell-tales of the time. The system was
developed in the 1680s and the account of watch no. 21
explains the invention.

Set-up
A device which alters the range over which the stop-work
allows the mainspring to operate. This could be a simple
ratchet to adjust the amount to which the spring is still wound
when the stop-work prevents further running. Worm-and-
wheel set up may have been designed to allow the owner of the
watch to fiddle with it with relative impunity.

Stackfreed
The main cause of inaccuracy in early watches was the great
variation in power output of the mainspring as it unwound to
drive the watch. A coiled spring produces its greatest energy
when fully wound and its energy output lessens progressively as
the spring uncoils. Because the balance in a watch has no natural period of swing its rate of oscillation is determined by its
mass, its radius, and the amount of energy imparted to it by the
escapement. This meant that, without some means of evening
out the force exerted on the oscillating balance by the mainspring via the train of gears and the escapement, the watch
would gain drastically at the beginning of its run and lose significantly towards the end. To ensure reasonable accuracy the
watchmakers in the Germanic states introduced the stackfreed,
a strong spring with a roller at its free end which acted on a
snailed cam geared to the mainspring arbor, pushing against the
mainspring to lessen its force at the beginning of the run and
acting with the mainspring at the end of its run to augment its
failing power.

Stop-work
A mechanism to limit the extent to which the spring can be

wound up or allowed to run down. Avoiding the two extremes, fully wound and completely unwound, greatly reduces the variation in the spring's force, helping to improve timekeeping. In stackfreed watches it consisted of a wheel with one uncut space which prevented the spring from either fully unwinding or from being fully wound up. In fusee watches, the stop-work consists of a stop-iron on the movement plate which intercepts a hook at the top of the fusee to prevent further winding. The watch cannot run down beyond the point where all the line or chain is off the fusee and back on the barrel, effecting the other requirement of stop-work.

Striking mechanism – nag's head
A system commonly found in earlier watches in which the striking mechanism is released by a twelve-point star-wheel mounted under the dial on the dial wheel. The nag's head is a triangular piece pivoted on the arm which releases the striking train. As the star-wheel rotates once in 12 hours, every hour a point comes into contact with the nag's head, and turns it against a spring until it meets a stop. The whole arm then begins to turn until the striking is released. The striking train then lifts the arm further, so the spring then flicks the nag's head behind the star wheel point which had been in contact with it, so that the arm is free to fall back into position until the process begins again for the next hour.

Tambour watch case
As the name suggests, it is a drum-shaped watch case with a base and cover. This style was popular in the mid-16th century in South Germany. However, by about 1580 it had ceased to be fashionable.

Up-and-down indicator
A device found in high-quality marine and pocket chronometers as well as top quality watches. It consists of a hand registering on a dial which indicates the state of wind of the machine, a series of gears linked to the winding system and an indicator scale and hand on the dial. When the mainspring is fully run down the hand will show 0 on the scale and when winding takes place the hand traverses the scale to show fully wound at

the end. As the machine runs so the hand traverses back across the dial to show how much running time is left. This was found to be extremely useful in marine chronometers, which had to be kept running constantly in order to determine the longitudinal position of the ship.

Volvelle

A device consisting of a fixed circle of calibrations over which is a manually turned disc with an aperture which, in practice, allows information engraved on the lower scales to be read in conjunction with information engraved on the rotating scale. The most common form is perhaps the lunar volvelle which shows the age and phase of the moon as it develops over $29\frac{1}{2}$ days.

Watch-paper

A printed paper disc which is usually placed inside the outer case of a pair-cased watch (q.v.) to act as a buffer between the two metal cases. In most instances, these papers were placed inside the watch as an advertisement for repair and cleaning services available.

Brief description of some of the scenes depicted on the watches

Diana and Actaeon
A scene from Ovid's *Metamorphoses* Book 3 in which Actaeon, whilst hunting in the forest, happens to see the goddess Diana and her hand-maidens bathing in a pool. As a punishment for looking at the naked goddess, she turns Actaeon into a stag whereupon he is hunted down and killed by his own hounds.

Narcissus
A young man who did not return the love which Echo had for him and who mocked other lovers. Subsequently, he saw a reflection of himself in a pool and fell instantly in love with it. However, not being able to receive any love in return from the reflection, he pined away and died.

Orpheus Charming the Animals
Ancient Greek legend tells of Orpheus, the son of Oegrus and the muse Calliope, who was the most accomplished musician and poet. His magical performance could charm wild beasts and cause rocks and trees to move.

St Stephen, The Stoning of
The story of the martyrdom of St Stephen, the first Christian martyr, is from the *Acts of the Apostles*, chapter 6, verses 1–15 and chapter 7, verses 51–60.

Susanna and the Elders
Two elders spied on Susanna whilst she was bathing naked. When confronted by her they threatened to black- mail her unless she offered them sexual favours. When she refused they accused her publicly of having committed adultery and she was condemned to be executed. The prophet Daniel, unconvinced of her guilt, decided to question the elders and on doing so he found such inconsistencies in their separate accounts that they were themselves condemned to death and Susanna was acquitted.

Bibliography

Abeler, Jurgen, *Meister der Uhrmacherkunst*. Wuppertal,1977.

Baillie, G. H., *Watchmakers and Clockmakers of the World*. London, 1969.

Baillie, G. H., *Watches, Their History, Decoration and Mechanism*. London, 1929.

Baillie, Clutton and Ilbert, *Britten's Old Clocks and Watches and their Makers*. 9th edn. London, 1982.

Breguet, Emanuel, *Breguet, Watchmakers since 1775*. Paris, 1997.

Bruton, Eric, *The History of Clocks and Watches*. London, 1979.

Camerer Cuss, T. P., *The Camerer Cuss Book of Antique Watches*. Woodbridge, 1976.

Cardinale, Catherine, *The Watch*. New Jersey, 1989.

Chamberlain, P. M., *It's About Time*. London, 1964.

Chapiro, Adolphe, *La Montre Française*. Paris, 1991.

Chapuis, Alfred, *La Montre Chinoise*. Attlinger, 1919.

Chapuis, A. and Jaquet, E., *Technique and History of the Swiss Watch*. London, 1970.

Clutton, C. and Daniels, G., *Watches, A Complete History of the Technical and Decorative Development of the Watch*. London, 1979.

Culme, John, *The Directory of Gold and Silversmiths, Jewellers and Allied Traders 1838–1914*. Woodbridge, 1987.

Cutmore, M., *Watches 1850–1980*. Newton Abbot, 2002.

Daniels, George, *The Art of Breguet*. London, 1974.

De Carle, Donald, *Watch and Clock Encyclopedia*. London, 1975.

Develle, E., *Les Horlogers Blésois au XVIe et au XVIIe Siècle*. Blois, 1917.

Edgcumbe, Richard, *The Art of the Gold Chaser*. Oxford, 2000.

Evans, J. *Thomas Tompion at the Dial and Three Crowns*. Antiquarian Horological Society. Ticehurst, 2006.

Gazeley, W. J., *Clock and Watch Escapements*. London, 1973.

Good, R., *Watches in Colour*. Poole, 1978.

Hayward, J. F., *English Watches*. London, 1979.

Jagger, Cedric, *The Artistry of the English Watch*. Newton Abbot, 1988.

Kemp, Robert, *The Englishman's Watch*. Altrincham, 1979.

Loomes, Brian, *The Early Clock Makers of Great Britain*. London, 1981.

Loomes, Brian, *Watchmakers and Clockmakers of the World*.Vol. II. London, 1976.

Meis, Reinhardt, *Pocket Watches*. West Chester, 1987.

Priestley, Philip, *Early Watch Case Makers of England 1631 to 1720*. Columbia: National Association of Watch and Clock Collectors' Inc. *Bulletin*, Supplement No. 3, 2000.

Priestley, Philip, *Watch Case Makers of England*. Columbia: National Association of Watch and Clock Collectors' Inc. *Bulletin*, Supplement No.20, Spring 1994.

Shenton, Alan and Rita, *Watches, 1840–1940*. Woodbridge, 1995.

Symonds, R. W., *Thomas Tompion, His Life and Work*. London, 1951.

Tait, G. H., & Coole, P. G., *Catalogue of Watches in the British Museum*, Vol. 1, 'The Stackfreed'. London, 1987.

Tait, G. H., *Clocks & Watches*. London, 1983.

Tardy, *Dictionnaire des Horlogers Français*. Paris, 1971.

Vial, E. and Cote, C., *Les Horlogers Lyonnais de 1550–1650*. Lyon, 1927.

Weiss, Leonard, *Watchmaking in England: 1720–1820*. London, 1982.

Index